Bearing Fruit

BEARING
FRUIT

SERMONS FOR CHILDREN

Harold Steindam

Illustrated by Marguerite Wilson

United Church Press

Cleveland, Ohio

United Church Press, Cleveland, Ohio 44115
©1994 by Harold Steindam

Biblical quotations are from
the New Revised Standard Version of the Bible,
©1989 by the Division of Christian Education
of the National Council of the Churches of Christ in the U.S.A.,
and are used by permission

99 98 97 96 95   5 4 3 2

Library of Congress Cataloging-in-Publication Data

Steindam, Harold, 1950–
Bearing fruit : sermons for children / Harold Steindam ; illustrated
by Marguerite Wilson.
p.   cm.
Includes index.
ISBN 0-8298-1013-7 (alk. paper)
1. Children's sermons.   2. Church year sermons.   3. Sermons,
American.   I. Title.
BV4315.S6844   1994
252'.53—dc20   94-35080   CIP

To my daughter, Sara,
Who, born "later"
In my life,
Could make me
Older sooner
Or keep me
Younger longer—
With thanks that she has chosen
The latter.

Contents

Introduction

During the time that I was studying for the ministry, I was asked to lead worship for a congregation whose pastor was to be on vacation that week. I mailed my order of worship to them in midweek, and on Sunday morning I drove to the church. As part of my order of worship I had listed a children's sermon; however, when I invited the children to gather with me, no one came forward. Not a single child was present that morning.

Granted, this was summertime, and even the pastor had chosen this to be a "vacation Sunday." Still, this was a larger than average congregation, meeting in a spacious sanctuary, and so this circumstance surprised me. Things worked out well enough, as I simply shared informally with the adults the ideas I had prepared to share with the children. However, it is not that morning itself, but what I thought and said later in response to the experience, that I wish to consider here. I found myself commenting to others that I was concerned about the future of that congregation because there had been no children present that day.

What I thought and said were by no means unique to me. My point of view is expressed quite often in the church. Certainly, in the twenty or so years since that experience of "worship without children," I have heard the same attitudes verbalized more often than can be counted.

"The children are the future of our church." "After all, the young people are going to have to carry on for us and be our future." "It's so good to see children coming up for the children's sermon, because it shows the future our church has."

These are but a few of the ways this attitude is expressed. They are all well-meaning statements, often made by the most caring of persons. Yet, if these statements reflect the full extent of our thinking, then we are greatly lacking in our embracing of the message of Jesus.

With this publication I complete a trilogy of books on children and children's sermons. Though each book has been written to be used over the course of a single year on the church calendar, the actual writing of each took about four years, so that the time from the beginning of the first to the completion of the third is more than a decade. During these years of watching, working with, and worshiping with children, I have found that not only have the children grown, but my understanding has grown with them.

For a long while I spoke and acted with those who say that children are the future of the church. However, I have come to realize how limited that thinking is. Stated simply and directly: Children are not the church's future, but an integral part of the church's present. Further, only if children feel accepted and valued for who they are in the present will they be likely to choose to be part of the church in years to come.

When Jesus declared to his disciples that they should let the children come and not hinder them, for such was the nature of the realm of God (Matt. 19:14), he was not referring to who those children would be in fifteen years, but to who they were on that very day. Likewise, when Jesus said we must be children to be part of that realm (Matt. 18:3), he was not talking about our past or a possible future, but about the present moment in our lives. Children matter—now. We must care about them and learn from them in ways that show this—now. This was and is the message of Jesus.

For too many years we have viewed children in worship much like the flowers that adorn the altar. We know they are made by God and are beautiful, but they are to be seen and not heard and certainly not involved as participants. Children must be seen and heard and entrusted with responsibilities in worship in order for the gathered congregation to be the body of Christ.

We hear frequently about the crisis in many of our churches in terms of numbers of children and youth who are involved. That church I visited twenty years ago seems, quite sadly, less and less unusual. The number of children in church school programs has declined, as have the numbers in youth activities and confirmation classes. It is further lamented that a majority of those in confirmation classes are seldom seen again after their confirmation day. I am alarmed by these numbers. I know that much of the decline can be attributed to demographic differences, with fewer children in most homes today. But this cannot explain away all that concerns me, and so I sympathize with those who tally the numbers and worry about the future of the church.

Many responses have been made to this matter. However, many of the attempts of recent years have not addressed the situation as they need to in order for us to be as Jesus would have us be. Any attempt to minister to and with children is doomed to limited success, if not outright failure, if it is conducted in a way that views children as potentials for the future rather than disciples of the present. Every youth program must see and celebrate that our children are today bearing fruit that is meant to be part of the harvest that Jesus saw and proclaimed.

We have hired youth workers and attempted to set up programs of all sorts for young children and teens in the church. This may appear to be the answer, except for the fact that often these additional staff members and programs have segregated the children from the rest of the congregation. The children go away—whether from the worship service or from the congregational activity or from the church building entirely—so that each group can do what it does without the presence of the rest of the body of Christ. These programs may be extremely well done, and the children may greatly enjoy them, but if this is the extent of their involvement, they certainly are not being thus prepared for a future in the church. Only as an activity enables children to see themselves as part of the church *now* does it lead to future involvement as well. Only when our children are seen to be important in worship now, only when confirmation programs are integrated into the life of the congregation now, only when the ideas and concerns of teens are seen as valuable to the direction of the church now, will the present trends that are so discouraging be reversed.

The children's sermon can be an important way to express our understanding that children are not simply the church's future, but very much part of its present life. In bringing this about, the approach of the leader of the children's sermon is all important. Certainly the leader will have an idea in mind for the time when the children come forward. But the leader's primary attitude must always be one of listening. In this manner he or she can truly move through this gathered time in response to the feelings and the spontaneous ideas of the children. A good leader is one who knows when to lead and when to allow the group to take itself in a new direction. A good leader hears and responds to genuine concerns and questions, learns to separate statements made only as attention-getters from those that are sincere, and knows how to respond appropriately to each. A good leader develops relationships that over time create an atmosphere that encourages open, honest, and respectful comments. Children recognize sincerity and concern, and when they feel listened to and valued—not only by the leader but by the congregation in whose midst they gather—they become aware of how special this time is, and they want to be present to share it each week.

Have you ever wondered why children wanted so much to be with Jesus? What was it that drew such a number to him and alarmed the disciples to the point of thinking they had to intervene and keep the children "over in their own area" until they were older? Surely something about Jesus drew children to him. What was so powerful was that he genuinely cared about them and listened to them and reached out to them for who they were as they gathered. Jesus recognized and celebrated the fruit they were bearing. The children responded. They wanted to be there to share the gift.

Not only have demographics changed over the past generation, the world has changed. We must change our attitudes to respond accordingly. Here is the crux of the matter. Children are born ever the same in a world that is ever different. Children are endowed with innocence, but live in a world that is far from innocent. In the church, more than anywhere else, we must recognize and find a way to deal fully with these polarized points.

As I think about my own growth of understanding over this past decade, I realize that I have grown most of all to see that the innocence of children is priceless, and that this innocence must be made to last as long as possible. That very innocence of children, which we can witness and share, is the sweetness of their fruit that we may taste when we are with them. The greatest thing that could happen in this world would be for all adults first to have a wonderful childhood, a wonderful time of innocence.

However, the world strikes out at childhood innocence, as we know all too well. It forces its way into children's lives in harsh ways. Sexually explicit media messages surround us, and the numbers of pregnancies and sexually transmitted diseases among adolescents are higher than ever before. Drugs and alcohol are introduced to children at younger and younger ages. Stories of crimes and violence, and about the destruction of our environment and the consequences of such actions, are heard almost daily. The pressure to be like others—particularly to be like the latest popular personality or fad—is greater than ever for our children and teens. It comes from the media and in the form of peer pressure among the youth themselves. Add to this the fact that there are many more broken families than there were a generation ago, and that children often are forced to divide their time between households or to try to blend into a new family, so that the stability needed to deal with such great issues can be difficult to find.

In the center of this polarization of children and the world, the church stands with the greatest and most important of messages in response. The church, with the loving words and example of Christ, can and must walk the thin line between such opposites, must find ways to enable the innocence of children even while being fully aware of and not afraid of the realities of the world in which children must live. The love of God shown in Christ is greater than any reality that will ever have to be faced. This above all is our message: God's love is greater than whatever we may face. Therefore, the church's leaders do not need to avoid certain subjects. We can face the harsh truth—when the truth *is* harsh—in ways that still allow for childhood innocence to be lifted up and celebrated.

As we see our children not as resources for the future but as vital members of the church today, we care about who they are and what their world is like. As we do this we harvest the fruit they bear today. Only in this kind of attitude and relationship will we have children who will grow further toward wanting to share those gifts and to face whatever must be faced with the generation who in turn will follow them.

This book contains ideas for fifty-two sermons for children, following the seasons of the church for a complete year. Each chapter is introduced with a scriptural reference. In some cases this scripture is specifically quoted or referred to in a general way in the sermon, while at other times it is not mentioned. In each case, however, the verse provides the context for the ideas within the sermon. Each leader can use the reference however he or she feels is best. In the worship bulletins at the church I serve, I have the text printed so that parents or teachers may have it in mind as they later talk with their children about the ideas we have shared.

Each of the fifty-two sermons also contains a brief statement of the basic concept it is meant to convey. The person leading the session needs to have the concept clearly in mind before the beginning of the time together, so that even when things do not proceed exactly in the order planned, the leader can guide the discussion toward the desired lesson.

Each of these sermons was written with—in my mind's eye—a circle of children around the leader. The text relates only the words of the leader; however, a good amount of dialogue takes place as the children feel free to offer their ideas.

Other forms of gathering better suited to the style of a particular leader certainly may be used. And these ideas may be used in one-to-one readings or sharings of a parent with a child, or in other gatherings in a home or church setting.

As noted earlier, my intent is for the love of God to be shared within the joyful innocence of childhood, and yet with a willingness to address the difficulties our world presents to children. While I have not dealt with every possible issue, I have addressed many, including concern about the environment, facing disappointments, the death of a childhood friend, dealing with disabilities, matters of race or color, drug abuse, and being part of a blended family. Also, issues including homelessness and AIDS are addressed as the children themselves bring them into the discussion.

This book is meant to be a primer, a beginning point for better understanding of what Jesus shared with us long ago: that our children are fully a part of God's realm for who they are right now; that we have been given much to teach them and they have been given much to teach us; that nothing can be more beautiful than what they in their freshness from God know in these present moments; and that there is nothing in this world that they and we, together in the love of God, need ever fear.

THE SEASON
OF ADVENT

1 · Hurry Up and Wait!

SCRIPTURE LESSON: *Jeremiah 33:14—"The days are surely coming . . . when I will fulfill the promise."*
OBJECT NEEDED: *A pizza delivery box*
CONCEPT: *The experience of waiting for Christmas, which may seem long and difficult, is a very important part of the full celebration of it.*

I have something to show you that I am sure you will all recognize. . . . Yes, it's a pizza box! We had pizza delivered to our house last week, and I saved the box to talk about with you. . . . What, Samantha? . . . No, there is no pizza in the box now. I'm sorry about that! Tell me, though, if there were pizza in here, what would you want to have on it? What are your favorite toppings? . . . Mmm, yes, pepperoni seems to be the favorite overall, and there are several votes for extra cheese, and one or two for mushrooms. . . . What, Sara? . . . Yes, if others in your family say they don't want their mushrooms, you get to pick them off and eat them. But please don't do that unless they say that you may!

Have any of you ever done what our family did last week? Have you ever called on the telephone and asked for pizza to be delivered to your house? . . . It looks as though just about all of you have. Last week, when we decided to order pizza, we were already hungry! So we hurried to decide what kind to get and we hurried to find the telephone number and we hurried to call the pizza place.

But then, do you know what? After we hurried and hurried, we had to wait and wait! It seemed as though we had to wait a very long time for the pizza to arrive. Have you noticed that, too? . . . Yes, when we are hungry and watching at the window, it seems to take a long time for that delivery person to finally come!

It can seem the same when we are waiting for Christmas to come. We feel that we are waiting and waiting, and we want it to be here soon, but it seems to take so long.

Today we have lit the first candle on our Advent wreath, and we are very excited to think that Christmas is coming. But look at how many more candles still must be lit. There are about three and a half weeks to go until Christmas. That seems like a very long time, doesn't it? . . . Yes Stephanie, I know. You want it to come fast, don't you, because there are so many wonderful things about Christmas that you are looking forward to!

I want to tell you something very important, though. This time of waiting and waiting is part of what makes Christmas so wonderful. We light one new candle each week, and we count the days on purpose, because waiting for Christmas and getting ready for Christmas is a great part of it.

In the part of the Bible before Jesus was born, the part called the Old Testament, people waited for a very long time for one to be born who would be their Messiah or Savior. They waited and waited, and then God's promise was kept and the special baby was born. That waiting was very important, because people would always remember how wonderful it was when the baby finally was born.

In the season of Advent, which we are beginning today, we wait and we watch and we pray, just as people a long time ago did. This time helps us also to know and to remember how wonderful it is that Jesus finally is born into our world.

Last week, when that pizza finally arrived at our house, it tasted so delicious! I think it tasted even better because we had waited and watched for it. Christmas also will come. It will because God says that it will. And at that time it will be even happier and better because we had been waiting and getting ready for it during each of these days of Advent. The birth of God's special baby is important enough for us to wait and to watch for many days, and then to be happiest of all when it finally happens.

3

2 · Give Me an "A"!

SCRIPTURE LESSON: Mark 1:2—"*See, I am sending my messenger ahead of you, who will prepare your way.*"

CONCEPT: *As we better understand the meaning of Advent, we are better prepared to experience the joy God wants us to know.*

Today two of our candles on the Advent wreath are lit, and that is great. That means that Christmas is getting closer, doesn't it? That makes me glad, and it makes me want to cheer! Will you help me do a cheer? . . . Let's do it! I'll be the cheerleader, and you shout back to me!

> *Give me an A!* (A!)
> *Give me a D!* (D!)
> *Give me a V!* (V!)
> *Give me an E!* (E!)
> *Give me an N!* (N!)
> *Give me a T!* (T!)
> *What does that spell?* (Advent!)
> *What does that spell?* (Advent!)
> *What does that mean?* (—!)

Wait a minute. We were doing so well until that last part. Maybe we should try it again. What does that mean?

Hmmm, I notice something here. We say this word "Advent" many times, but we don't know exactly what it means. Let's talk about this and try to understand. Advent is a word that was made by putting two Latin words together, and those two words mean "coming toward." Think about that. We are coming toward something so wonderful that an entire season is named for it. What do you think we are coming toward right now? . . . Yes, Jake, of course. We are coming toward the birth of Jesus, and Advent is the time of the year that we think about that and prepare for it in special ways.

Today we have lit the second candle on our Advent wreath. The second candle is meant for us to think about John the Baptist. It was John the Baptist's special job to get everyone as ready as possible for Jesus, to "prepare the way" for him.

That is a job that all of us can do, too. We are to be like John the Baptist and help to get everyone ready for Jesus to come. We do that by talking to people. We do that by singing the songs of Christmas. We do that by choosing gifts for others as a way of telling them how much they mean to us. We also prepare for Jesus to come to be with us by being extra kind and helpful to people who are in need right now.

From now on when someone asks us what Advent means, we can answer that it means we are coming toward something very wonderful— toward the birthday of Jesus. Remember, also, that we can each be like John the Baptist and help to get ready for that wonderful event. By learning what the words and customs of the season mean, and by doing all we can to prepare for Jesus through loving words and actions, we can make our Christmas celebration this year the most wonderful time of all.

3 · Welcome Inn!

SCRIPTURE LESSON: *Luke 2:7—"* . . . *because there was no place for them in the inn."*

CONCEPT: *The most important part of our Christmas preparation is opening our hearts to receive Jesus.*

Today is the third Sunday of Advent, and our Christmas pageant is fast approaching! Superintendent Becky tells me that everyone has been working very hard on the program that will tell us the wonderful story of how Jesus was born.

This morning I want to share with you a story of what once happened in another church when their children did their Christmas pageant. In that church each child had a part to play, as many of you will. Some were angels and some were shepherds, and there was a person to play Mary and someone to play Joseph. Also, in that church's version of the play, there was someone to act out the part of the innkeeper.

We remember that the inn was completely filled with people by the time that Mary and Joseph arrived in Bethlehem. So the only place for them to stay was in the stable with the animals. That was the place where Jesus would be born. Well, this church chose a boy named Tommie to play the part of the innkeeper. His job was to tell Mary and Joseph that there was no room in the inn, but that if they wanted to they could stay in the stable. Then Mary and Joseph would go over to the manger, where the rest of the play would take place.

At the rehearsals, Tommie did his part perfectly. He always told Mary and Joseph that there was no room, and that they could stay in the stable. Then Mary and Joseph would move on for that next, important scene in the play.

Then the day of the play arrived. On this day everyone was in full costume. All the parents and other family members and friends in the church were there for the performance. Everything was going perfectly in the play as Mary and Joseph came to the inn and Tommie, playing the innkeeper, answered their knock at the door. A special spotlight was shining on Mary and Joseph, and Mary was dressed to look as though she was going to have a baby very soon. The boy playing Joseph said his line— that his wife was going to have a baby and that they needed a place to stay. Tommie listened . . . and he looked at Mary . . . and he thought—and suddenly he said, "There's no place in the inn, but you can have my room!" Then he opened the door and let them in!

Well, what do you think about what Tommie did? Do you think he ruined the play by not saying his line and doing what he was supposed to do? . . . Yes, in one way he did, didn't he? . . . But, what? . . . Yes, Gregory, I think you have a good thought there. Tommie said something that was very wonderful, because in that moment he just couldn't send Mary and Joseph away, could he? He felt something in his heart and forgot to say his line, and instead said what he was feeling.

Tommie invited Mary and Joseph in because he wanted the baby to be born in his own room! That is a wonderful lesson for all of us as we get ready for Christmas.

When the play was taking place at Tommie's church, what he said and did caused a few difficulties at first, but then they went on and played the scene the way the Bible says it really happened. But since that time the people there have always remembered what Tommie said, because what he said is what the innkeeper could have said, and it is what all of us can say to be as loving as God wants us to be. . . .

Do you have an idea, too, Lynley? . . . Yes, you are right! That is a wonderful idea, and one that I had not thought of. Right now our church is working to help a homeless family from this community to be able to have a home again, and there is a great similarity to this story. And, yes, as we think about homelessness and what a problem it is that so many families do not have homes, it is good to remember that Mary and Joseph were also homeless people for a while.

You have given us all much more to think about! Thank you. Let's think about Lynley's idea, and remember the story I told today, and all think more about how we can say "Come right in!" the way Tommie did. By caring about others and sharing with them, we are able to know all the Christmas joy that God wants us to know.

4 · Be Our Guest!

SCRIPTURE LESSON: *1 Corinthians 16:22—"Our Lord, come!"*
CONCEPT: *As we anticipate and receive Christmas, we allow Jesus to come into our daily living in new and wonderful ways.*

Four candles are burning on our wreath today. This is exciting because Christmas is now only a few days away!

What I would like to talk about with you may not seem like a Christmas idea at first, but I hope that you will see that it is. I want us to think about the prayers we say. Especially, I want us to think about the prayers we say before we eat. Do any of you ever say a prayer at your dinner table before you eat? . . . It seems that many of you do.

There are some prayers that have been thought up just for mealtimes, ones that children often learn and say. Have any of you learned a prayer like that? . . . Could you tell me a prayer you have learned? . . . "God is great. . . . " Yes, Rachel, thank you. That is a wonderful prayer to say. Are there . . . yes, Katherine? . . . Oh, yes, that is the one I learned to say when I was growing up: "Come, Lord Jesus, be our guest."

Tell me what you think it means when we say, "Come, be our guest" to Jesus. What is a guest? . . . Yes, it is someone who visits us. Sometimes we have guests at our home for a meal. Do you ever have guests at your house for dinner? . . . Yes, Grandma and Grandpa, and cousins—they are wonderful guests to have! When we have guests for dinner, we set a place at the table for each one of them, don't we? Each one gets a plate and a cup and silverware and a chair.

Well, if we pray to Jesus to come and be our guest, as Katherine does, what does that mean? Should Katherine set an extra place at the table with an extra chair for Jesus? . . . If we don't do that, then do we still think that Jesus hears our prayers and will be there with us? . . . Yes, Michael, we still think so, but it is in a different way, isn't it?

We want Jesus to be our guest at the table and at other times, too. We cannot see Jesus the way we see the other people who visit us, but we know Jesus is with us because God sent him to us out of the greatest love of all!

With Jesus as our guest at the baseball field or at school or when we are with our friends or our family, we can remember to be kind and fair and to do our best always. That is what it means to have Jesus as our guest, because Jesus helps us to see and to know what God wants for us.

All through this Advent season we have been getting ready for Jesus to come to us. We have been praying for Jesus to be our guest. Now Christmas is almost here, and we know that Jesus will come to us in new and wonderful ways and be a guest in our lives not only on Christmas Day, but on every day, wherever we are, whatever we are doing. "Come, Lord Jesus, be our guest," we pray. And he does just that! Because of Christmas we know that Jesus is our guest wherever we are or will be!

THE SEASON
OF CHRISTMAS

5 · A Silent, Wonderful Gift

SCRIPTURE LESSON: *Luke 2:46—"They found [Jesus] in the temple, sitting among the teachers, listening to them."*
CONCEPT: *One of the most precious gifts we can give is that of listening; when we give that, we also receive great blessings.*

Whew!

Do you know why I said that? I said that because now Christmas Day is past—and what a busy time we had leading up to it! We did so much shopping and decorating and wrapping. We went to many worship services and programs and parties. And we received presents in abundance. Did each of you receive a special present this year? . . .

Well, again I have to say it! Whew! Yes, many wonderful things have come to us through these recent days and weeks.

The other day—just the day after Christmas—I was at a friend's house, and we began to talk about the gifts that we had given or received this year. All of a sudden it was so noisy in that house! It seemed as though everyone started talking at once. But then I noticed my friend's little girl, because she was listening carefully and trying to pay special attention to each person near her who was talking. That was so wonderful that I found myself wanting to get closer to her and talk more with her. As I did, and as it felt so good to talk to her, I realized that she was giving one of the most wonderful gifts anyone can ever get. She was giving the gift of listening, of really caring about what each person said.

Our scripture story is one that you may already know. It is the only story we have of something Jesus did when he was a child, and so it is very important to us. When Jesus was twelve years old, his family made a trip to Jerusalem and went to the temple, which was what they called their place of worship. Jesus wanted most of all to be with the teachers there. Our story says that he listened to these teachers. Then he asked questions and listened some more to their answers.

What a wonderful thing that is for us to learn and know about Jesus—that he was a good listener.

As we have now shared all the wonderful joys that lead up to Christmas—and we have given and received so many gifts—we come to a more quiet time of the year. Now come days that are more restful, days that give us more time just to think—and to get ready for the new year that soon will begin.

As we have been thinking about gifts so much lately, I want to say to you today that one of the best gifts of all, one that we can give all year, is the gift of listening. Being a good listener, really caring about what another person is saying, paying attention to what that person is feeling and means to say—what a wonderful gift that is! There is such need in our world today for people who carefully listen.

Besides being a wonderful gift, listening also helps us to receive. When we listen, we come to learn and understand so much. That is why Jesus wanted to listen carefully. He wanted to learn all that those persons could teach him.

What a wonderful example it is for us to read that Jesus as a boy wanted to listen and to learn. I am glad for that story. I am glad for the Christmas season we are having and for what will continue with us into the new year ahead. I am thankful for each one of you, and for the ways you can be good listeners, and for the ways that this gift lasts, not just for a season but for all of our lives.

. . . What, Amanda? Yes, you have been good listeners today! I thank you for that wonderful gift.

---

6 · *Just a Minute!*

SCRIPTURE LESSON: *Isaiah 49:8—"Thus says [God]: 'In a time of favor I have answered you.'"*

OBJECTS NEEDED: *A stack of paper tablets with a total of 1,440 sheets of paper*

CONCEPT: *God gives us all the time that is ours; it is up to us to use that gift in meaningful ways.*

Happy New Year to all of you! Yes, early in January we all think about the new year that God has given us. At this time of the year especially, I think about how much time God gives us.

January is the first month of the year. How many more months will there be this year? . . . That is right, because there are twelve months in a year. How many days are there? . . . Right, there are three hundred and sixty-five, although in leap years there is an extra day. . . . What, Paul? You want to figure out how many hours there are this year? . . . And you have your calculator with you? Okay, what do you figure? . . . If you say 8,760, I believe you! How did you get that number? . . . You multiplied

14

the number of days times the number of hours each day! You have learned very well from your math teachers, haven't you?

I want you to think about another number today, a number that also is very big. I want you to think about minutes, and how many there are in each day. First of all, tell me how long a minute is. . . . Yes, it is sixty seconds long. Now give me an idea of how long that is by telling me something you can do in a minute. . . . You can give your mom and dad a hug and tell them you love them! Thank you, Julia, I like that! What else takes about a minute? . . . You can pet your cat . . . feed your fish . . . take your plate from the table to the sink. Those are all things that take only a minute or so.

Now I want us to think about another big number. Do you know how many minutes there are in a day? There are twenty-four hours in each day and sixty minutes in each hour . . . and that equals 1,440! I was thinking about that number this week, and I wanted to find a way to show you how big that number is. So I started to count the sheets of paper in some tablets that I have. The stack of tablets finally got to be this big, just by showing how many minutes there are in every day, with one sheet for each minute. I hope that you will remember how this looks and how many minutes God gives us every day.

Maybe some of you will want to try this at home or with friends, to find a way to show how many minutes there are in every day. I hope you continue to think of all the wonderful things you can do in those minutes of each day that God gives to you. Every minute is like a clean sheet of paper, because it is new and we can use it however we decide.

We are thankful to God, who has given us this new year with all of its months and weeks and days. Remember that every day is made up of so many minutes, and think of all the good ways we can use those minutes. How glad I am for the gift of every minute we have—because each is from the God who loves us so much.

THE SEASON
OF EPIPHANY

7 · Beholding What the Light Reveals

SCRIPTURE LESSON: *John 1:9—"The true light, which enlightens everyone, was coming into the world."*
OBJECT NEEDED: A *light bulb*
CONCEPT: *God has come to us in Jesus, and in the season of Epiphany we celebrate all that Jesus shows us.*

One night this week I came home and found no lights on anywhere in my house, so I could not see anything! I even felt a little bit unsure and cautious in those moments. But then I did something that we often do when we walk into the house or into a different room. Do you know what that was? . . . Yes, Jenna, I flipped a switch. A light came on and I could see everything in the room, and then I did not feel unsure anymore.

Light bulbs do something very wonderful, don't they? They light the rooms of our homes and schools and other places we go. When we switch the light on, it shows us all the things that are in the room that we could not see before. These things do not suddenly come into the room. Nothing is there that was not there before, and nothing goes away that was there before. The light just shows us the truth about what is there.

What I tell you next may sound funny at first. It is that our eyes cannot see light itself. Can you believe that? . . . Well, it is true. We are not able to see light itself. Instead, we are able to see things *because of* light. Let me say that one more time. We cannot see light itself, but we are able to see the things that light falls upon, the things that light shows to us. When I turn the light on in my home, I am able to see the chair and the desk and the carpet and the pictures on the wall—all the things that the light touches and reveals. Here in this room right now I am able to see the flowers and the communion table and the hymn books, and I am able to see each one of you. I am able to see all this because light is in this room and is falling on all these different things and on each of you. And I am so glad for the light! How beautiful everything looks today, and how especially beautiful each one of you looks to me today!

We are beginning a new season of the church year today, and this season is called Epiphany. It comes just after Christmas, when we are happy that Jesus has been born and is with us. One of the important symbols for Epiphany is light. We feel as though a light has been turned on and we are now able to see and be glad for many wonderful things. We know there is no need to be frightened or unsure, and we can he happy and glad about God's love. Many scripture verses tell us this. One of my favorites says that Jesus is the true light who has come into the world and helps us all to see because of that light.

I told you that we cannot see light itself, but we can see all the things that light shines upon and shows to us. The same is true about Jesus. We cannot actually see him with our eyes, but we can see everything he shines on. Since Jesus came to us on Christmas, and since he is with us now, we know how much God loves us, and we know that we do not have to be frightened about anything.

We see the world God has given us—and we see all the special people that God has put into our lives. As we think in this season of Epiphany about all that God has given to us, and about how we can see it because of the light of Jesus, we give thanks in joyful celebration!

---

8 · The Times of Our Lives

SCRIPTURE LESSON: *Acts 16:15—"When she and her household were baptized . . ."*

OBJECT NEEDED: *A picture—at as young an age as possible—of the leader of the session*

CONCEPT: *When we baptize infants or small children, it is with the understanding that God loves them even before they know it, and that they will grow always more in God's love.*

I want to show you a picture this morning. I'll hold it and walk slowly about so that each of you can look at it. . . . What does this picture show? . . . Right, Michael, it is a baby. Do you know who the baby is? . . . No, that is pretty hard to say, isn't it? But I know who this is. It is a picture of me when I was a baby! I was only about three months old at this time. Let me hold it up right next to me. . . . Now can you tell? . . . Well, maybe and maybe not! When you know who it is, then you can see some similarities, but I certainly have changed since this picture was taken, haven't I? The same is true for all of you. You each have changed so much since you were babies, and you will change much more still.

Even though we change as we grow, and even though we look different and learn many new things—even so, there is still always something the same. My whole life I have been only one person—and that is also true for you. This is a picture of who I was and how I looked a long time ago—but I was that person.

Today has been a very happy day at our church, because we have had a baptism in our congregation. Michael's baby sister, Rachel, was baptized just a few minutes ago. I know that Michael and Rachel's parents brought a camera so that they will be able to take a picture of Rachel before they leave today, a picture that will always show how she looked on her baptism day.

Someday Rachel will look much different than she does today. She will know and do many things that she can't today. And yet, she is one person. Who she is, who God made her to be, will always be the same. She is Rachel, and will always be Rachel.

Some people wonder why we baptize such little babies at our church. After all, Rachel does not understand that she has been baptized today. She will not even remember it. But we chose to baptize her today because she has been born into a family that knows that even though she does not know about God yet, God already knows and loves her completely. And so she will always be growing in that love, always learning more about God in her home and here at her church, because she lives in a Christian family.

Someday Rachel will be able to say yes for herself to all these things that her family has said for her today. It will be wonderful at that time when she will confirm those things for herself. But she will never need to be baptized again. Each person needs to be baptized only one time in her or his life, because we are always the same person. Rachel is and always will be Rachel, a person made by our Creator God, loved by our Savior Jesus Christ, and cared for by the Holy Spirit that is always with us.

We change so much. We grow and we learn. We look very different as time goes by, and this picture that I am holding is a good reminder of that. God is happy about all those wonderful changes, because that is how God made us to be! But even though we change, something always stays the same. We are always one special person whom God has loved since before we even knew it. That is why we are so happy today, as Rachel has been baptized. We are happy that God loves Rachel completely, and that she can come to know that love more and more as she learns and grows, just as each of you, so loved by God, can learn more and more every day as you change and grow—and yet always stay that same person that God loves so much.

---

9 · Sisters and Brothers All the Same

SCRIPTURE LESSON: *Luke 19:9—" . . . because he too is a son of Abraham."*

OBJECTS NEEDED: *Baseball cards*

CONCEPT: *The brotherhood and sisterhood Jesus proclaimed goes beyond skin color and other outside differences.*

Do any of you like to collect baseball cards? . . . Wow, just about all of you do! I'm not surprised. My children like to collect them, and so did I when I was growing up. I wish that I had saved all those cards I used to have!

I want to tell you about a girl who collects baseball cards, and about the talk she had with her father one day. She was looking at her cards and reading the names of the different players, when she saw two that had the same last name. First she saw this card, with a picture of Bo Jackson. Then she saw this card, with a picture of Danny Jackson. The little girl was so excited that she ran to show them to her father. She said, "Oh, Dad, do you think they could be brothers?" Her father looked at them and said, "Well, even though they have the same last names, Bo and Danny aren't related. Some people might think that they're unrelated because they are not of the same race. But this isn't necessarily true." The little girl thought for a moment, and then she said, "So they could still be brothers anyway?"

What do you think? Could they still be brothers? . . . Yes, Kara, I believe you are right. They can be brothers—even in a more important way than growing up in the same family would be. I like the story of the little girl with her baseball cards, because she had an idea that is very much like something that Jesus taught. Jesus taught that all of us are sisters and brothers, because God is the parent of us all.

This week we remember and celebrate the birthday of a man named Dr. Martin Luther King, Jr. . . . Have you learned about him at school, Krista? . . . Yes, Dr. King talked about the dream he had for a time when all children could play together and be friends, no matter what their race. He spoke about a time when all people would know they are brothers and sisters and would think most of all about the love inside each other, not about race.

Dr. King did not just think up these ideas. He found them in the Bible in the teachings of Jesus. But we honor Dr. King because he did so much to help us realize how these teachings can become true for our lives each day.

We can be brothers and sisters to each other by caring about each other, by being kind to each other, by being friends to each other. When we do that, we are sure to feel happy and to know how God wants our world to be.

As we remember Martin Luther King's birthday, this is the best way to honor him, by remembering what Jesus taught about being sisters and brothers to each other. I hope you will remember the story of the little girl and the baseball cards. Maybe you can even tell it to some friends.

I wish all of you, my sisters and brothers, a very happy Martin Luther King holiday!

10 · What Difference Can I Make?

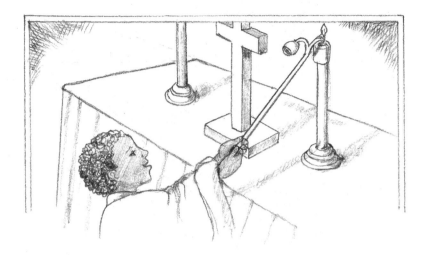

SCRIPTURE LESSON: *Isaiah 11:6—"And a little child shall lead them."*
CONCEPT: *Children play a very important part in our worship of God.*

I am glad that our church has the tradition of letting children take turns being acolytes. Some of you have done this job for us, haven't you? I would like to talk with you about what happens—and what it means—as our acolytes do their important job for us.

As the music begins to play at the start of our worship service, our two acolytes come up the aisle. Their candle lighters are lit, and that shows us how God's light comes into our place of worship as we gather here. They light the candles on the altar. . . . Yes, they are burning right now and will burn throughout the worship time. All the while these lights remind us that God is with us. Then, as we sing our final song of worship, the acolytes come forward again and do something that is very important. First they relight their candle lighters from the candles that have been burning on our altar throughout worship. Then they put those candles out. Finally, they carry their lighted candle lighters back down the aisle where they had come in at the beginning of worship. This reminds us that we are to go out from worship and carry God's light into the world, into all the places that we will go in the coming week.

That is a very important job, and I am glad for each one of you who does this job for our church.

We are now in the season of Epiphany, and light is one of the most important symbols of this season. During Epiphany we give thanks for the ways that God has come into our world and into our lives through Jesus, and for all the wonderful things we are able to see because of Jesus, whose light shines on us and on our world.

Light is a very important symbol for God. The first words God said at the beginning of creation were "Let there be light," and with those words all of creation began. Every time we worship our wonderful Creator, we begin with light. We begin worship by having acolytes come up the aisle and light the candles—and children of our church do this very important job.

One of my favorite verses in the Bible tells us that children will lead all people to discover and learn what is most important from God. I am glad that in our church one of the ways that we show this is true is by having our children do the important job of carrying God's light into the sanctuary to begin worship—and then carrying it out from the altar after worship to show that we all need to follow and help carry God's light into the world.

Some of you have already had turns doing this, and others will get to do it some day. Thank you for the important ways that you lead all of us to see what God wants us to see. Thank you for all the things you do at our church and in all other places you go as you spread God's wonderful light for others.

11 · P.S. I Love You

SCRIPTURE LESSON: *1 Corinthians 16:24—"My love be with all of you in Christ Jesus."*
OBJECTS NEEDED: *Magnets and hand-drawn pictures*
CONCEPT: *It is important to express how much we love each other in ways that are noticed each day.*

Many times I visit someone's home and notice that this person or family has an art museum right in the house! Can you believe that? They really do! They have a whole museum of drawings and paintings on display, and they are all held up by one of these. . . . Yes, Kenny, these are magnets, and the place where these great paintings are displayed—which I call an art museum—also serves as the family's refrigerator!

Here are some examples I borrowed from one of these art museums that I sometimes visit. Look at these. . . . Aren't they wonderful? Why do you think these are put on the refrigerator for display? . . . That is right, Mark. These are pictures that have been drawn by the children or grandchildren of these families. Do any of you have pictures like these on your refrigerator? . . . Oh, good. . . . Many of you do. Travis says that his grandmother puts up pictures he draws for her. That is great . . . and Sarah says when she gets an extra good paper in arithmetic, her parents put that up. . . . What, Michelle? . . . Oh, there are pictures of *you* on the refrigerator at some houses, too! That is also wonderful for an art gallery.

The question I want to ask most of all is "why"—why do people put up these drawings or homework papers or pictures? What is the reason? . . . Yes, it is because they love you. And so, everything about you is important. Putting these things up to be seen is a way of showing how much you are loved.

There will be a holiday in this coming week. . . . Yes, it is Valentine's Day! And what is Valentine's Day about? . . . It is about love. It is a day to tell special people we love them. Many of us will send valentines to friends at school or to other special people, or we will do things to tell others that we love them.

Valentine's Day is a wonderful holiday. It is a great idea to have a holiday for telling others we love them. But we do not have to wait for Valentine's Day to do that. Jesus has taught us that every day is a day to tell others how much we love them. Every day is a day to treat special people in ways that tell them they are special.

One of the most important followers of Jesus was a man named Paul. Paul wrote many letters to people who were special to him. Many of those letters were so good and so important that they became a part of our Bible! In almost every one of his letters, Paul ended by telling the people he was writing how important they were. It was as if he always remembered to say "P.S. I love you."

I am very happy for all the ways we can tell others how special they are and how much we love them. I am glad for refrigerator art museums that many of you have at your homes, or at the homes of your grandparents, or of aunts and uncles. Every day those things are on display to remind us of how special we are to each other, how much we love each other.

I am glad that every day can be like Valentine's Day when we follow what Jesus has taught us. Most of all, I am glad for each one of you—for how special you are, for how much you are loved, by me and by so many other people, too!

12 · Whistling While He Worked

SCRIPTURE LESSON: *John 8:32—"And the truth will make you free."*
CONCEPT: *Honesty brings many rewards.*

A friend of mine told me about a job he had a long time ago, when he was about the age that some of you are now. A man in his neighborhood had several cherry trees, and when the cherries were ripe he hired my friend to pick them. One unusual request went with the job, however. My friend was told that while he was picking the cherries, he would have to *whistle*! The owner of the trees said he would be a little distance away and would be listening to hear if my friend was whistling the whole time!

Wasn't that silly? Why do you think he asked such a thing? Why did he want my friend to whistle while he worked? . . . Oh, you figured it out, didn't you?

You see, the year before my friend also had been hired for this job of picking cherries, but he had spent much more time eating than he had picking. So now the man who owned the trees wanted to know that my friend really was working and not eating, and as long as my friend was whistling, the man knew that he couldn't be eating at the same time.

I can understand what he was thinking, but it would have been best of all if the man had known to begin with that he could trust my friend. Every job or situation is better when people are able to trust each other.

Tomorrow we will celebrate a holiday called Presidents' Day. One of our most important presidents was the first one, George Washington. There are many stories about George Washington, including the one about him and a cherry tree. Do you know that story? . . . Loren, why don't you tell it to us? . . .

You say that when George was honest about what he had done—admitting that he had chopped down the cherry tree—his father did not punish him. His honesty was more important than anything else. That is the lesson of that story, and it is one I am glad our children learn in school as they grow up.

One of the most important things any of us can do is tell the truth. When we tell the truth, and people know that we do, we can all work together or play together or learn together, and we can all do so much more and so much better.

One of the most important things Jesus taught us is that the truth makes us free. Everything else is like a trap because there is always something wrong with it that will cause problems later.

It is wonderful to know that we can be truthful about everything because the most important truth of all is that God loves us and cares about us as we live every day. That is why Jesus said that the truth will make us free.

I hope you will remember the story of my friend and how the man thought he could not be trusted, because it shows how things are not right when we think we can't believe someone. Remember that as you also remember the story of George Washington this Presidents' Day. And most of all remember that the truth sets us free, because the truth is that God loves us and cares about us in all that we do every day.

THE SEASON
OF LENT

13 · Marching to a Different Drum

SCRIPTURE LESSON: *Mark 1:13—"[Jesus] was in the wilderness forty days."*
OBJECT NEEDED: *A newspaper clipping or chart that shows the times of sunrise and sunset for the coming week*
CONCEPT: *The season of Lent (which means "lengthen") is a time to become closer to God through Jesus.*

Today is the first Sunday of what Christians believe is the most important season of the year. . . . Yes, Amanda, this time is called Lent. I want to talk with you about why this season has the name that it does, and why it is so important to us.

First of all, I want to show you this chart that I made. It tells what times the sun will be rising each morning and setting each evening in the coming week. We can see that every day this week the sun will rise one or two minutes earlier and will go down one or two minutes later. Every day will be a little bit longer as the sun will be with us a little more every day. Even though it is still winter, we know that spring is coming. Every day during winter is a little bit longer than the day before, until we come to the first day of spring, when the time between sunrise and sunset will be exactly twelve hours—which is half of our twenty-four-hour day. Then the daylight will continue to increase until the first day of summer, when we have the longest time of daylight for the whole year.

Now that I have reminded us of what is happening with the daylight right now, can you figure out why this season of Lent has the name that it does? . . . Very good, Aaron. . . . Yes, that is the idea. We call this season Lent because it sounds like the word "lengthen." The days are lengthening, meaning that they are getting longer. At this time of the year we know that spring will soon be here, and along with spring comes our celebration of Easter.

A long time ago Christians wanted to have a time to get ready for

---

Easter, so they began to plan a special season to prepare themselves for it. They decided that this season should have forty days in it because there had been an important time in Jesus' life that lasted forty days. For forty days Jesus thought and prayed, to try to be closer to God. During Lent we count the forty days from Easter—plus Sundays—backwards to begin the season we call Lent.

People who believe in Jesus as their Savior want to make this the most meaningful time of the year, and they do things that will help them to feel closer to God, as Jesus did. Some people do extra reading of the Bible or spend more time in prayer. Others try to do a kind act for someone every day. Still others give up eating something they like during Lent. I have one friend who does not eat chocolate during Lent, even though he likes it very much. He says that this helps him to think about all the things that Jesus gave up for us. . . . Yes, that is not an easy thing for all of us to understand, but it is something that we can think more about.

I have tried to explain about quite a few things today. Let me tell you one more time about the ideas that are most important. I want you to remember that we are now in the season of Lent, and that we call it that because the days are lengthening as we get closer to springtime. Lent is marked on the calendar for forty days plus Sundays before Easter. Finally, and most important of all, Lent is a season in which followers of Jesus do things that will help them feel closer to God through Jesus. By doing that, they will be able to have the most wonderful celebration of Easter.

In the season of Lent, Christians try especially to follow the way that God directs them, as Jesus did, by knowing that God is with us and God loves us every day.

14 · A Cross All Our Days

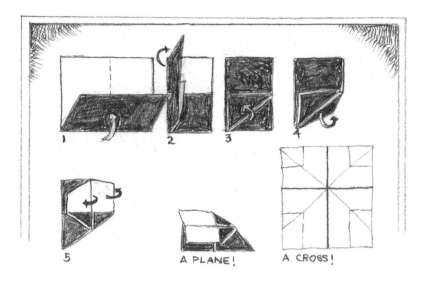

1   2   3   4

5   A PLANE!   A CROSS!

SCRIPTURE LESSON: Mark 8:34—"If any want to be my followers, let them . . . take up their cross and follow me."
OBJECT NEEDED: A paper airplane folded to show a cross within it
CONCEPT: As followers of Jesus, we are to think each day of how we can follow the way of life he showed us.

Today is the second Sunday in the season of Lent. We have learned that Lent got its name because this is the time of the year when the days are lengthening. Today I want to talk with you about what this season means. In the Lenten season we are to think about all that Jesus did. Especially, we are to think about how he died on the cross for us, and how he wanted his followers to live. One of the things that Jesus taught is that we each must have a cross in our lives if we are going to be his disciples. That is a very great and difficult teaching for us.

I want to show you something. With this piece of paper I am going to fold . . . an airplane, . . . and I am going to fold it in a certain way . . . like this. . . . You can see that on the outside it looks like any paper airplane. But inside there is more to it. Look at this . . . and you can see that when I unfold it the lines from the folds inside . . . show a cross to us. . . . Yes, I will be glad to do it again and show you how it is made. . . .

On the outside a follower of Christ may look like anyone else. But on the inside, a Christian always remembers how Jesus taught us that to be his followers we must live as he did. We must be truthful. We must care about others even when it is not easy. We must do all that we do knowing that God loves us and is always with us. And as Christians we think every day of how Jesus died on a cross for us.

Followers of Jesus see things differently. They may look the same on the outside, but inside something is different. This paper airplane looks the same on the outside, but inside there is something very different: a cross.

As Christians, we see the cross of Jesus in what is inside us, because as followers of Jesus this is important to us. Especially during the season of Lent we want to think about this and about all the good that we can do when we live the way Jesus has shown us.

During the season of Lent, we try to be more like Jesus, which is not always easy. Every day, it means making life the best it can be for ourselves and for others. On the outside we may look the same as anyone else, just as this airplane looks like any other paper airplane on the outside. But inside this airplane—and inside each of us—there is the outline of a cross. Because Jesus loves us so much, we also can love. Learning more about how to live that love each day is what the season of Lent is about!

15 · Getting Inside the Matter

SCRIPTURE LESSON: *Matthew 23:25—"For you clean the outside of the cup . . . but inside they are full of greed."*

OBJECT: *A cup like the one Jesus describes, clean on the outside, but with dried chocolate syrup inside*

CONCEPT: *Just as a cup needs to be clean on the inside even more than on the outside, so do we. That is what our prayer of confession can do.*

I have a special cup that I like to use. Do any of you have a cup that is your favorite? What does your favorite cup look like? . . . I can understand why each of those is special. Here is my favorite cup. It has a picture of my favorite team, the Detroit Tigers, on it. This cup has been my favorite for many years, and I like to keep it looking as nice as I can all the time.

Look at how clean it is! It almost shines, doesn't it? When it is on my desk or at my table, that shine on the symbol of my favorite team is important to me. . . . What, Josh? What did you notice? . . . You say there's stuff inside my cup? Yes, there is. That's just some chocolate syrup, because yesterday I mixed chocolate milk in my cup. But I don't worry about that. Almost nobody sees the inside, so that doesn't matter, does it? . . . What do you think, Bailey? . . . You think that I could get sick if I don't wash the inside of my cup better? That's right, because germs grow in places that are not clean. It is good that I keep the outside of my cup looking nice so that other people can see my favorite team's symbol shining so brightly. But it is much more important to have the inside clean.

There are many ways that we can clean the outside of our bodies, and that is important. We wash our hands and take baths, and we keep our clothes clean. But there is another kind of being clean that is even more important, and that is on our inside. We need to feel close to God and to know that God loves us all the time. We have all done something that wasn't right at times, and we need to know God understands and forgives

---

us. We also need to know that we are going to keep doing our best for God all the time, wherever we are. Knowing these things gives us the happiest feeling there is!

In our worship service today there was a part called the prayer of confession. That is not easy for us to understand, but here is part of its meaning. We cannot wash the inside of ourselves with soap, the way we can the outside. But praying the prayer of confession is like helping the inside of us become cleaner and better. We tell God we are sorry for any ways we have made God sad, and we promise God that we are going to do our best from now on. We then think about how much God loves us, and that helps us to feel so much cleaner and better. After all, we know that God has already sent Jesus to us! That's how much God loves us!

From now on I am going to be very careful about washing the inside of my cup, because that is the most important of all. When that is taken care of, then I can also take care of the outside. And I am going to think about how much God loves me, even when I have done something that makes God sad. I am going to think about how the inside things that I know and feel are even more important than what is on the outside of me. My cup helps me to remember that the most important things are on the inside! And I am glad, because that is where God loves each one of us most of all!

---

16 · A Penny's Worth

SCRIPTURE LESSON: *Matthew 10:29—"Are not two sparrows sold for a penny?"*
OBJECTS NEEDED: *A penny for each child*
CONCEPT: *God's care gives us our value, no matter what may happen in our lives.*

I have something for each of you this morning. It is a gift, but I have to admit it is about the smallest gift I could give you. It is . . . a penny! Here is a penny for you, Amber . . . and for you, Brianna . . . and one for everyone else, too. . . . Tell me, what can a penny buy? . . . Well, there are a few things, but not too many.

Pennies used to buy more than they do now. Perhaps you could talk to your grandparents about what they were able to buy with a penny when they were children. Pennies have always been one of the smallest amounts of money. That is true today; it was true when your grandparents were growing up; it was also true back when Jesus lived!

In Jesus' time there were people who sold sparrows. It is difficult for us to understand, but back then people used animals in their worship of God. Sparrows were one of the most common, ordinary kinds of birds then, just as they are now. The cost of a sparrow was a penny apiece or three for two pennies. To buy one sparrow cost one cent, but if a person paid a second penny the storekeeper would give a second sparrow plus another one. So, in a way, that third sparrow did not cost anything. It had no worth at all, not even a penny!

But Jesus talked about the third sparrow as a way of telling us how great God's love is. Jesus said, "God loves every sparrow—even that one that is given out for free!" And then Jesus said, "If God loves sparrows that much then just think about yourself, and about how much more God loves you, and think about how much God is going to take care of you!" Jesus said that God knows things about us that we don't even know about ourselves—like how many hairs are on each of our heads, and all the things that happened to us when we were babies and we can't remember!

Something is printed on every one of our pennies. Perhaps some of you can find it and read it along with me. It is on the side of the penny with Abraham Lincoln's face on it. The words are "In God we trust."

What a wonderful thing that is to say. On this smallest of all coins, we find this message that is the most important one there could ever be. It is the message Jesus wanted us to learn when he taught about sparrows and about God loving us even more. "In God we trust." We can trust, and we can be sure, because God loves us and is watching us always.

There are times I do not feel happy or good about myself. There are times when something causes me to be afraid. But God is always with me and loving me. That is the wonderful message Jesus wanted every one of us to understand and remember.

I hope the penny you have received this morning—and each penny you get or use—will remind you of this wonderful teaching of Jesus. Yes, we can all feel trust and joy because God loves each one of us so much, and loves us all the time.

---

17 · Not Giving Up

SCRIPTURE LESSON: *Philippians 3:14—"I press on toward the goal."*
OBJECT NEEDED: *A picture of Michael Jordan*
CONCEPT: *As we try our best, God is with us, and good things come to us from God.*

Do you know who this is? . . . Yes, almost all of you do! Amanda says this is a picture of Michael Jordan, and she is right. What is Michael doing in this picture? . . . That is right, David. He is jumping high into the air and is just about to slam dunk the basketball through the hoop! This is an amazing picture, because it shows an amazing basketball player in action. Many people believe that no other player in the history of basketball has ever been as good as Michael Jordan. I agree with them. When he was at his best, he did things that no other player could do. He also helped his team win three straight professional championships.

We see Michael Jordan's picture many places. We see films of his basketball plays over and over on television. We hear him speak about many different things on all sorts of commercials and programs. Just about everyone agrees that he is the best basketball player ever.

There is something else, though, that is a very important part of Michael Jordan's story. It is not something that everyone knows, but I think it may be the most amazing part of all.

A long time ago, when Michael Jordan was in high school, he decided to try to be on his school basketball team. At his school, as at many schools, only so many kids would get to be on the team, and more than that came to try out for it. So the coach had to watch everyone practice and play and then decide who would be on the team.

And do you know what happened? That year, when Michael Jordan first tried to be on a high school basketball team, he was told he was not good enough. . . . Isn't that hard to believe? . . . But it is true. The person that we now know as the greatest player ever was once told he was not good enough to be on a regular high school team.

When Michael went home that day, how do you think he was feeling? . . . Yes, I agree with you. I am sure he felt very sad, and maybe he was thinking that he would never get to be on a team and never be a very good player.

It would have been very easy for Michael to decide that day that he would just give up trying. After all, he had been told he was not good enough for the team, so why should he bother to keep trying?

But that is not what Michael did. Instead, he went home and he practiced even harder. He did not give up, even though he was disappointed. When the next year's team was being picked, he came back and tried again. And this time he made the team! He had practiced and grown and improved—and he didn't stop trying to improve. We all know how good he came to be after that, and some people think that part of the reason he became so good is that he never stopped trying and trying. Even when he was the best player on the Chicago Bulls team, he still practiced more than anybody else. He would often be the first player to get to the gym to practice his shooting, and he would always try to be a little bit better.

There are many things that we can say about Michael Jordan. But I want to be sure that you remember this part of his story. Whenever you see a picture of him or hear someone talking about his great career, I want you also to remember the disappointment he felt when he was told he could not be on his high school team. Remember also how he would not give up, and how he always tried his best for the years he played.

We can set goals and try our best, too. When we do that, then whatever talent God has put inside us will come out, because God is with us as we do our best. I am glad that Michael did not give up when he was discouraged. I am glad for how you keep on trying to do your best, too.

41

18 · God's Care for All

SCRIPTURE LESSON: *Job 39:19—"Do you give the horse its might? Do you clothe its neck with mane?"*
OBJECT NEEDED: *Something that shows an animal's natural protection*
CONCEPT: *God shows special care for every creature. Jesus knew and trusted in God's care, and so can we.*

I have something to show you this morning, something that looks very strange. . . . It is a kind of fish. It is called a puffer fish, and this fish does two things to protect itself from enemies. . . . First of all, it puffs itself up. That is why it is called a puffer fish. When it puffs itself up, it looks much bigger than it actually is. That way it scares enemies that are fooled into thinking it is too big to go after. The second thing that happens is that when it puffs itself up, these little spikes on its body stick straight out. That makes it much more unpleasant for a bigger fish or sea animal to think about eating. . . .

One of my favorite books in the Bible is the book of Job, and in it God talks to Job about all the things that God does to take care of our world and those who are in it. In this book it tells how God has given special qualities to every animal that has been created.

As I think about this fish and what it has for protection, I find myself thinking about other animals. It is true that every animal has some special quality that helps it take care of itself. Let's think about some. . . . What about a turtle? How are turtles protected? . . . Okay . . . and rabbits . . . yes, by being fast runners. Birds can fly . . . and insects cluster in huge swarms to protect themselves.

What other animals can you think of that are protected in special ways? . . . Very good!

What about people? How are we taken care of and protected? . . . Yes, we are bigger than many animals . . . and we can run or are strong in some ways. But most of all . . . yes, we have the greatest intelligence! We can learn things and we can remember what has worked in the past, and we can take care of ourselves by thinking and then doing what is best.

I said that the book of Job is a special favorite of mine. It also was one of the books that Jesus knew and read as he grew up. Jesus learned about how God takes care of all of the creatures of the world—especially people. Through this book and in many other ways, Jesus learned to trust in God and in the care that God gives to all of us.

By trusting in God always, Jesus was able to do many wonderful things. And the same God that Jesus knew and trusted also loves every one of us. We, too, can trust God and know that God will always care for us. That is good news—wonderful news—to remember as we use the wonderful minds and bodies that God has given us for our special care each day.

THE SEASON
OF HOLY WEEK

19 · Bracing for Whatever Must Be

SCRIPTURE LESSON: *Isaiah 40:1—"'Comfort, O comfort my people,' says your God."*
OBJECT NEEDED: *A child's leg brace or something else that is used to correct a physical problem*
CONCEPT: *We all face times or situations that worry us, but God is with us and helps us to face whatever must be.*

This week I took these things out of one of our closets. I do this every so often. I take them out and look at them and think about them for a while.

These are two kinds of braces for very young children. This one is a hip brace, and these are ankle and foot braces. When my son Nevin was very small a doctor discovered that a bone in his hip was not growing correctly, so for five months he had to wear this brace. Later, shortly after my son Caleb was born, we learned that his ankles were not growing correctly, and so he had to wear these braces on his feet and legs for three months.

It has now been more than ten years since either of my sons had to wear these braces. I am very happy that each one grew as the doctors had hoped he would and that we could take off the braces for good.

As I said, that was more than ten years ago. I have kept these braces all these years. The braces were made exactly to fit each of them, so they cannot be used by anyone else. But I keep them and look at them and think about them every so often.

Why do you think it is that I do this? Why do you think I keep these? . . . Yes, those are good answers to my question—and my question is not an easy one at all. I have kept these braces because they help me to remember what I was thinking about and what worried me at the time my sons had to wear these. I worried about whether their bones would get better. I worried about how it would be if they always had to wear braces. And sometimes I wondered how God could let this happen.

I look at these braces now and I am very thankful because my sons' bones did grow correctly. These braces help me to remember how thankful I was when each boy could take them off for the last time.

Usually things end up working out well. We get sick, but then we get better. Sometimes we have to move to a new place, but then we make new friends and are as happy as we were in the old place. Sometimes children have to wear a cast or a brace or be in a wheelchair for a while, but then they get better and do not need those things anymore.

Sometimes, though, problems do not get better. Does anyone here know someone who must always use a brace, or must always be in a wheelchair in order to go places? . . . Do you, Darci? . . . Yes, and probably all of us know people who wear glasses or a hearing aid, or something else that helps them in some way.

No one has a body that works perfectly. Everyone needs help to do better or to feel better sometimes. I am very glad for all the things that can help people when they are in need, whether it's just for a little while or for all of their lives. I am glad because I know God wants us to feel well and to be able to do our best.

That is why I have saved these braces. They remind me of how much God is with us and takes care of us. They remind me of all the things that God has helped us to learn to make and to do in order to help people.

20 · When Butterflies Aren't Free

SCRIPTURE LESSON: *Mark 9:31—"Then [Jesus] began to teach them that [he] must undergo great suffering."*
OBJECT NEEDED: *An empty cocoon or a picture of a butterfly*
CONCEPT: *Certain things can come to be only when we first go through a time of struggle. This was true for Jesus, and may also be true for us.*

I have an empty cocoon case here, and you can see the hole where a butterfly got out. I remember a time when I was walking in the woods and I came upon a butterfly that was trying to get out of its cocoon. I was amazed. I watched the butterfly struggling and struggling to get out, and I began to wonder if it would ever be able to do it. Finally, I decided I would help the butterfly, and I began to look for a stick to break a bigger hole for it, so that it would be able to get out more easily.

Fortunately, though, I was with a friend who knows much more about nature—and about butterflies—than I do, and he would not let me help the butterfly. He told me that if I broke the cocoon open for the butterfly to get out easily, it would probably die that very day. He told me that the hard work and the terrible struggle that the butterfly goes through are very important. All of that work—all of that flapping of wings that the butterfly has to do to get out—makes it strong enough to be able to fly. Also, there is a kind of oil on the butterfly's body that works its way out and onto the wings of the butterfly as it struggles inside the cocoon. By the time the butterfly gets out, the oil has gotten all over its wings, and that protects it from the outside air. Without that oil, the dry air and the dirt outside will cause the butterfly's wings to get weak and to crack, and so it will die without that protection.

"You see," my friend told me, "God has made the butterfly in such a way that it feels trapped inside the cocoon and wants so much to be free that it is willing to struggle and struggle to get out. That very act of working and struggling prepares it to be free and to live in the outside world."

That is quite a lesson, isn't it? There are some ways in which we can be free only if we struggle in order to do so. Some good things can happen only if hard things happen first.

In the Bible story we hear today, Jesus talks to the disciples about how he will have to struggle and suffer. They want to help him. They want to keep him from doing any of those hard things. That is how we usually think, and it is usually a kind thing to think. But in this case Jesus tells them that only by first going through these very hard times will he then be able to rise from the dead and do the best things of all that God has planned.

Just about everyone has to go through something that is very difficult at some time. There are times when we have to struggle and suffer, when we wonder if we will ever be free. But remember the butterfly. Remember what God promised and did through Jesus. Remember that some things can come to be only after we have first gone through a time of struggling. Then—after that and because of that—we can truly be free and full of joy in all the ways that God wants for us.

THE SEASON
OF EASTERTIDE

21 · One, Two, Three on Me!

SCRIPTURE LESSON: *Matthew 28:5, 9—" 'I know that you are looking for Jesus.' . . . Suddenly Jesus met them."*
CONCEPT: *Jesus died and rose from the dead on Easter; his disciples
found him and the good news of God's love began to spread.*

Does anyone here ever play the game of hide and seek? . . . It looks
as though everyone does! This is a game that children have enjoyed for
years and years.

Let's talk for a minute about how hide and seek is played. One person
is "it." Let's pretend that person is Chad. Chad would cover his eyes and
count to a certain number. During that time all the rest of us would run
and hide somewhere. Then what happens? . . . Yes, Ashley, Chad would
look for us, and if he found one of us he would call that out. If he found me
he would shout "One, two, three on Pastor Harold!"

When I was a little boy and played this game, I had one really good
hiding place, so good that no one could ever find me there! But do you
know what? I stopped hiding there! I stopped hiding in that place because
it was too good. I realized that the most fun thing about hide and seek is
that moment when we are found! Everyone shouts and runs and cheers at
that time. It is so exciting. If no one was ever found, hide and seek would
not be very much fun, would it?

Today is Easter Sunday. It is an exciting day, and the most joyous day ever. Jesus had died, and his body had been put in a cave in a garden. In a way, he was hidden from his friends, and some of them gave up and did not look for him anymore. But there were some special friends who did not give up, and they went out early on Easter morning. And they found him! It was the most wonderful discovery of all—because Jesus was not dead, but alive! He had risen from the dead, showing how great God's love is and that God's love is even greater than death.

The most wonderful thing about hide and seek is the moment of being found. The most wonderful thing about Easter day was the moment of finding Jesus—and finding that he was no longer dead, but alive. On Easter, many of us hunt for eggs or other hidden things, because the happiness of finding those hidden surprises reminds us of the happiness of that moment of finding Jesus, and finding out the good news of how great and how wonderful God's love truly is.

This is Easter—and it is such a happy day! I am glad for all the happy things that you are doing at your homes and that we are doing at our church today. I want you to enjoy today, and I want you to think especially today about how much God loves you.

From now on, whenever you play hide and seek, or whenever you look for someone or something and find it, I hope that exciting, wonderful moment will remind you of the happiness of what was discovered on Easter Day, and of what we can rediscover every time we think of the good news of Easter.

22 · Seeing Double

SCRIPTURE LESSON: *John 20:24—"But Thomas (who was called the Twin), one of the twelve, was not with them when Jesus came."*

OBJECTS NEEDED: *Twins, or a picture of twins*

CONCEPT: *All of us are fooled sometimes, so we want to be careful about what we believe. We know that we can believe most of all that Jesus has risen from the dead.*

Have any of you noticed how often I get Stephanie and Melissa mixed up? Even though I have gotten to know them well, and they are my special friends, I am confused many times and call one or the other by the wrong name. That is because they are twins, and even though they are two different people and each a special individual, they look so much alike that I can be fooled about who is who.

Sometimes, I have noticed, they even *try* to fool me! And they do a pretty good job of it, too! They remind me of friends I had while I was growing up, twin boys named Ron and Don. They also fooled people many times into thinking that each was actually the other!

Today, for our scripture story, we hear about Jesus' disciple Thomas, who was a twin! The Bible says that he was called the Twin, so he must have had a brother who looked just like him.

Thomas came to have another nickname, too. Do you know what that was? . . . Yes, he was later called Doubting Thomas. After Jesus rose from the dead on Easter, he came back to visit his disciples. Everyone was there to see him except Thomas, and when Thomas heard about it, he just couldn't believe it!

I wonder if this was partly because Thomas was a twin, and because perhaps he and his brother had often fooled people about who was who. Maybe he thought the other disciples were just teasing him or trying to fool him when they said Jesus was alive.

Just a few days ago was April first, and many people played April Fool's jokes on each other. We all try not to be fooled, don't we? We want to be careful about believing things that turn out to be silly or not true. Now think about what the disciples were asking Thomas to believe. It is about as hard to believe as anything could ever be—that Jesus, who had died, was not dead anymore—that he had come back to life because God loved him—and loves all of us—so much.

That is a very big thing to believe, and it is only natural to wonder about it. But Thomas believed with all his heart when Jesus came to visit him and show him that it was true.

When I think about Melissa and Stephanie, or when I think about some of the ways I was fooled into believing things on April Fool's Day this year, I think about how careful we all want to be about things we believe, just as Thomas was.

Then I think about the story of how Jesus rose from the dead on Easter, and about how that is as hard to believe as anything could ever be. But we know it is true because God promised that it would happen, and people saw Jesus and knew for sure it was so. Even Thomas, who was very careful because he was a twin and knew about fooling people, came to know that it was true!

What wonderful news it is to know that Jesus really is alive again. We can believe it! No fooling!

23 · Recycling Hope

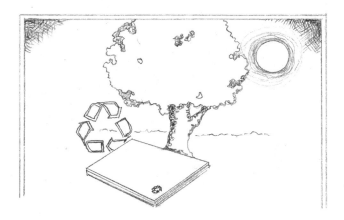

SCRIPTURE LESSON: *Job 38:37—"Who has the wisdom to number the clouds? Or who can tilt the waterskins of the heavens?"*
OBJECT NEEDED: *Something made out of recycled materials*
CONCEPT: *We care about our environment; with God's blessing upon our caring, good will come for our world.*

I want to show you something that I just bought for my office that makes me feel happy. It is a pad of paper. It may not seem so fantastic, but there is something different about this pad of paper.

Jeremy, I know that you are learning to read, and I'll bet that you can read what these words at the top of the pad say. . . . That is right. It says, "Made from 100 percent recycled fibers." That means that this pad of paper was made of all recycled materials. In my work in my office, I write many things, and I use a great deal of paper. Recently I learned about a new store that sells paper that has been recycled, and I plan to use this kind in my office from now on.

This makes me very happy. And do you think you know why? . . . That's right, Courtney. It makes a big difference to use recycled paper products, because it means saving trees! Paper is made from trees. I often think about how much paper I use, and I feel sad to think of how many trees were cut down in order to make that paper. Recycled paper, however, is made from paper that has already been used, so new trees do not need to be cut down quite as often. That makes me very happy!

We hear the word "ecology" used many times these days. Can any of you tell me what it means? . . . Very good, Amy. And Ken, what do you think? . . . Yes, ecology means the care of all our natural world—the air and water and soil, and the plants and animals, too. Many people are worried about our world . . . . Do you worry about it, too? Why would so many people be worried? . . . Yes, there is so much pollution . . . and litter . . . and you have heard about the hole in the ozone layer . . . and about too many trees being cut down.

There are many reasons to be concerned about our world. Some people make gloomy predictions and say that everything will get even worse by the time that you grow up.

I want to tell you one story, though, that gives me hope. When I was your age, I lived near Lake Erie. As I was growing up, the lake was getting dirtier and dirtier, because so many things were being dumped into it. There were always dead fish lying along the shore, and finally it was decided that Lake Erie was too dirty for us to go swimming in anymore.

It was then, about the time that I was in college, that some scientists said that we might as well consider Lake Erie dead. Nothing we could do would ever make it clean and nice again, they said.

Well, during that time laws were made so that companies—and people—could no longer dump whatever they wanted to into Lake Erie. People cared about it and helped to clean it however they could. And guess what? In just a few years the lake was getting clean and beautiful again! Even though many people—including some experts— thought it could never happen, it did! I am happy to say that I have been back in Lake Erie's water many times since then.

That is a story of hope for me. Whenever I hear gloomy predictions about our world, I think about Lake Erie, and I think about what wonderful things can happen when we give nature a chance again. If we all work together to not litter, and to recycle, and to use recycled products, and to plant more trees, and to clean up our world however we can, we will be amazed by what will happen. God, who made this world so beautiful to begin with, will bless our efforts with wonderful results.

There is reason to be concerned about what is happening. But there is no need to give up hope. We can make a difference—because God wants us to make a difference. That is why I am happy about these recycled pads of paper, and for all the other things that can help, even a little bit. All of us, working together with God the Creator, can help make this world even cleaner and nicer when you are grown up than it is now.

---

24 · Would You Mind?

SCRIPTURE LESSON: *Deuteronomy 5:16—"Honor your father and your mother . . . so that your days may be long and that it may go well with you."*

CONCEPT: *When children obey their parents not because they feel forced to do so, but because they choose to, they receive many blessings from God.*

Today I want to tell you about a family that I know. There are two boys in this family, and when they were little, their father died. Ever since then, their family has been made up of the mother and her two sons. When the father in this family died, the boys were five years old and seven years old. The mother was this tall . . . and the five-year-old was this tall . . . and the seven-year-old was this tall. . . . At that time, when the mother told her boys to do something, they would mind her and do it.

It has been about eight or nine years since the boys' father died. Today they both are teenagers. Now the mother is still this tall . . . just as she was back then. But now the younger son is this tall . . . and the older one is this tall! . . . Yes, both boys are now bigger than their mother. But do you know what? The other day I was visiting at their house, and the mother asked each of them to do some things. And every time she asked them, they did what she asked. Even when they did not feel like doing that particular thing right then, they still minded.

I have been thinking about this and trying to figure out why it would be. After all, each boy is now bigger than his mother, and she is not strong enough to make them do anything they don't want to. Can you help me to understand why they obey her even now, when they are so big?

Yes, Sasha, you are right. It is her house. So if they want to eat there and have a room there, they had better mind! You are right about that. But could there be more reasons than that? . . . I like that answer, Adam. It is because they love her, and they know that she loves them . . . . Yes, Ben, that is also true. She has lived longer than they have and understands many things. She asks them to do certain things not just because she wants them to, but because she knows it will be good for them. Yes, that is so. Parents do ask their children to mind them because they love them, and because they want what is best for them. Then, when the children follow these loving instructions, the best of things come to them. There truly are rewards that come to us when we honor our parents. Honoring means respecting, listening, and following their directions that come out of love.

Today is Mother's Day. Do some of you have special plans for your mothers today? Don't tell me anything that will ruin a surprise! . . . Oh, Amanda, your family made breakfast in bed for your mother! That is great— and it is something that already happened, so we didn't spoil any surprises, did we?

I am glad for a special day to tell our mothers how much we love them. But on every day, not just on Mother's Day, we can tell our mothers this, because every day their love is important in helping us to grow the way that God wants.

I hope you will remember the story that I told you about my friends, and about how the boys in that family mind their mother even now that they are bigger than she is! They mind her because they love her, and because they know that she loves them and wants what is best for them. And as they mind her they are blessed by God in good and wonderful ways.

25 · How Love Multiplies

SCRIPTURE LESSON: *John 6:9—"There is a boy here who has five barley loaves and two fish. But what are they among so many people?"*
OBJECT NEEDED: *A toy or other object being donated for people in need*
CONCEPT: *What we have to give may seem small compared to the great needs of others; however, God's love multiplies what we give so that there is enough for everyone.*

This morning I looked in the box of toys that we have been collecting, and I was glad to see how full it is! We have been hearing about the places that have been flooded and about all the homes that have been covered with water. That is very sad, because when water comes into a house, it ruins many things.

Many of the toys of the children who live in the flooded homes have been ruined. That is why we have been collecting toys at our church this week, so that we can send them to those children.

Here is one of the toys, a stuffed bear. . . . What, Edmund? . . . Was this your toy? That is wonderful. . . . And Heather, I see that you brought a toy today to put in the box. That is wonderful, too! Tomorrow we will take all the toys and pack them in boxes and send them to the children who need them.

Last night I was watching the news, and I saw how many houses have been flooded, and I thought of all the children who need toys. After I saw those pictures on television I looked at our box again, and I could see that there are not nearly enough toys in it to give to everyone who needs one. There are hundreds, maybe thousands as many children in need as we have toys. Still, we will send these toys that we have been collecting, and I believe they will make a difference for some of the children.

One of my favorite stories about Jesus tells of a time when many people—thousands of them—had come to listen to him. After a long time everyone was getting hungry, and the disciples started to worry about what could be done to feed all those people. Then one little boy came forward and gave Jesus the lunch that he had brought to eat. It was only five loaves of bread and two fishes. Everyone wondered what good that small amount of food could do when so many people were hungry. But because the boy had shared so kindly, Jesus took that food and he prayed, and he had his disciples pass it out to everyone. And, somehow, a miracle happened. Somehow there was enough food for everyone. That was the miracle of sharing, and the miracle of God's love shown in the kindness of sharing.

The same thing will happen with the toys you have given. Like Jesus, we choose these gifts and we pray to God and we send them on. Other children in other places also are sharing and saying prayers for what they have given. And every gift of love is blessed and multiplies, until there is enough for everyone who is in need.

Thank you for all the toys you have given or may still give, because every present given in love helps there to be enough. Just as the boy who gave his food saw it multiply enough to feed many people, that also will happen here. Thank you for your love, which is multiplied through God's love, which will help those people in need right now.

26 · Opening the Gates, One by One

SCRIPTURE LESSON: *1 Corinthians 3:2—"I fed you with milk, not solid food, for you were not ready for solid food."*

OBJECT NEEDED: *A small, adjustable fence used to keep young children confined to a certain area*

CONCEPT: *As we grow, we become ready for more and more opportunities and responsibilities. Waiting until we are ready for each new stage is a protection and a wonderful part of God's plan for us.*

Can anyone tell me what this is? . . . Yes, Ashley, it is a little fence, and it has a special job to do. Do you know what job this fence does? . . . That is right, Samson. It keeps small children from going into certain rooms or sections of a house. This fence can be made into different sizes, depending on how wide the doorway or other area to be blocked may be.

The job that this particular fence has been doing lately is to keep a little girl named Carly from getting into the room of her big brothers, Cole and Chase.

Do you think that Carly's family is being mean to her by not letting

---

her into her brothers' room? I know that she would like to get in there! Why do you think that her family keeps her out of their room with this fence? . . . That is exactly right! It is because her parents are taking care of her! There are many things in her brothers' room that could be dangerous to Carly. There are things that would be too sharp for her to use, or things that she might try to swallow and that would make her choke.

This fence is a kind of protecting love for her right now. Someday, when she is a little older, this fence will have another job. Maybe it will be given to a different family with a younger child.

A few months ago this fence blocked off the stairway, because it was not safe for Carly to climb or go anywhere on the stairs. Now she can go upstairs, and only the boys' room is blocked from her. Someday she will be allowed to go into their room, and perhaps then they will only have to block off the closet, where most of their toys for older kids are kept. Then, one day, they will not need a gate anywhere.

God has made us in a wonderful way so that as we grow, we become ready for more and more kinds of things. What may be dangerous for a smaller child is not a problem at all for an older one. And so we learn and we grow, step by step, stage by stage. And, slowly, the fences move back and then move back some more as we become ready for more responsibilities.

I am glad for the ways that each one of you is growing. I am glad, also, for how you help watch out for the younger children here at our church or at your school or in your neighborhood. I am glad for the fences that help us. They are helpful, because they protect us until we are ready to move on to the next area of learning and adventure that God will soon make possible for us.

27 · Not God's Will

SCRIPTURE LESSON: *Matthew 18:14—"So it is not the will of [God] in heaven that one of these little ones should be lost."*

CONCEPT: *God's will is not to take children from life, but to have children live and grow happily and healthily. When something happens that goes against that will, we mourn, and God mourns with us, and in open and honest facing of our sorrow we are comforted by God.*

This week has been a very sad one, hasn't it? I know that many of you knew Brett, who died so suddenly on Monday. Some of you, I know, were even his good friends, as my son Caleb was.

Brett was in the third grade, wasn't he? And his teacher was . . . who? . . . Oh, yes, that's right. And we all knew that Brett had missed a few days of school the week before with the flu, hadn't he? It seemed he would get better, because almost everyone gets better from the flu. But suddenly the kind of flu that Brett had went into some very unusual kinds of complications, and when his parents realized this and told the doctors, they did everything they could to help him. They even put him on the helicopter to take him as fast as possible to Children's Hospital, didn't they? But even with all the wonderful doctors who are there, and even with all the great equipment and medicine that they used, Brett still died. What had happened to him was just too sudden and too severe.

As I said before, when we get sick like that, we almost always get better. And more and more people all the time are able to get better because of all the medicines that God helps people to discover. But every once in a while, something happens that we cannot help. We do everything we can, but sometimes someone's life cannot be saved, and that is what happened in this very unusual situation with Brett.

There is no way for us to put into words just how sad and how awful this is. All of us who knew Brett are so sad that we wonder if we can ever feel better. Many of us—children and grown-ups, too—have cried and cried because what has happened is so terrible.

I want you to know that God hurts, and that God is crying with us right now, too. Some people think that God must have decided to have Brett die. But I want you to know for sure—*for sure*—that this is not so. Jesus said that it is not God's will for any child to die.

God wants children to grow up and to have long and healthy and happy lives. Sometimes very bad things happen—a disease or an accident, maybe—that cause a child to die. And that is so sad. It hurts God, as it hurts us. Another important thing that Jesus teaches us is that when such a sad thing happens, that little child becomes an angel who is extra close to God in heaven. I want you always to remember these things: remember that it is natural and right to feel like crying; remember how sad God is along with us; and remember that God has brought Brett to be extra close in heaven. I also want you to know that it is good to talk about your friend and always to remember him, and to know that even though you hurt so much and miss him so much, God is going to help you slowly to feel better.

I know that the whole school was closed on Thursday afternoon, so that children could go to Brett's memory service. . . . Yes, I know that many of you were there, and I am glad that you went. And what else is being done at your school to remember Brett? . . . Yes, a special tree will be planted, and a marker telling about him will be put in front of your school. That is a very good thing . . . . What, Kelly? . . . Yes I do want to hear what you are thinking . . . . Some people have said that you will forget about Brett after a while, but you and your friends have promised that you will think about him every day, always? . . . I think that is good, and I believe that you will remember him always. As you do the things that you know he liked to do, sometimes that will make you feel sad, but sometimes it will make you feel happy, as you remember how much fun you had with him.

Thank you for listening and for talking about this with me today. It is not easy to do, because it is so sad. But we feel better if we talk about it, and we know that we can talk about it because God is with us and loves us, just as God is especially close to Brett and loves him. We know how sad God is, just as we are, but we also know that God will help us always to remember Brett, and even to feel happier sometimes when we remember and do things we used to do with him.

THE SEASON
OF PENTECOST

28 · Caught by the Wind

SCRIPTURE LESSON: Acts 2:4—"All of them were filled with the Holy Spirit."

OBJECTS NEEDED: A hair dryer and a Ping-Pong ball

CONCEPT: On Pentecost the disciples received the Holy Spirit, which is the power of God's love that is with us now. The Holy Spirit cannot be seen with our eyes, but we can see what it does in people.

I have some things with me today that probably all of you have in your homes. First of all . . . I have a hair dryer. I have attached it to a long cord so that I can turn it on right now! . . . No, I'm not going to dry anyone's hair today, but I am going to do something with this. Here is a light, plastic ball, and I'll hold it above the blowing hair dryer and then let go . . . Look! The ball is floating! How can that be, when we can't see anything touching it? . . . Yes, Megan, it is floating on the air, on the wind, that the hair dryer is blowing. Can you see the air? . . . No, you can't. But you can see what the air is doing, can't you? Air does so many things! We cannot live without it. But our eyes cannot see it. We can see what it does, even though we cannot see the air itself.

Today is an important day in our church. It is Pentecost Sunday. Pentecost means "fifty days." It has now been about fifty days since Easter, when Jesus rose to new life from the tomb where his body had been put after he died on the cross.

About fifty days after the first Easter, Jesus' disciples were all together. They were missing him and wondering what God would do next. What God did next was send the Holy Spirit to them! We read in the Bible that the Holy Spirit sounded like a powerful wind that was blowing around them.

The Holy Spirit is the name for God's special power of love that we can feel inside ourselves right now. It is like the wind. We cannot see it, but we can see what it does! We also cannot see love, but we can see all the wonderful ways that love helps people.

On Pentecost Sunday we celebrate that the Holy Spirit has come to us. We celebrate that people are changed when God's Holy Spirit comes into their lives. We cannot see the air, and we cannot see the Holy Spirit. But we can see what the air does, and we can see what God's Holy Spirit does.

Perhaps you can show your friends the trick of blowing air from a hair dryer to hold a ball up, even though nothing else is touching it. Then you can talk about the difference the air makes, and the difference God's Holy Spirit makes in our lives.

I am glad for this happy day of Pentecost. This is the day that we celebrate and give thanks for God's Holy Spirit. We are thankful for the power of God's love and for all the wonderful things we are able to do because of it.

29 · Better Seeing Our Invisible God

SCRIPTURE LESSON: *Romans 5:5—" . . . because God's love has been poured into our hearts through the Holy Spirit that has been given to us."*

OBJECT NEEDED: *A three-leafed clover*

CONCEPT: *God, who is invisible to our eyes, has come to us in three forms, each helping us to know and understand better how much God cares for us.*

Whenever I see a patch of clover, I always try to find one with four leaves. Do you know why? . . . Yes, Claire, it is because many people think that four-leafed clovers are good luck. They are very unusual and difficult to find; so anyone who does find one is lucky. That must be how that idea about them started.

I like four-leafed clovers, but I have also been learning more about regular clovers. How many leaves do clovers usually have? . . . Yes, except for those unusual four-leafed ones, clovers have three leaves. God still has made each of them in a special way, with different patterns or shades of green and white on them. That is an important lesson for us to remember—that God makes every living thing in a special way. If you hold any two clovers next to each other, you will see what I mean.

I want to talk about another lesson from the clovers. The people of Ireland many years ago began to use shamrocks—which grow in their country and are similar to clovers—as a symbol of God. The shamrock also has three leaves, and those three leaves remind them of the three persons of God.

Just last Sunday we celebrated Pentecost, which is the celebration of the beginning of the Christian church after the Holy Spirit had come to Jesus' disciples. The followers of Jesus came to realize then that God could be understood in three different ways. As we look at the three leaves of this clover, let's think about each one of those important ways of looking at God.

First of all, God is the creator of us all. God is therefore like the most loving parent that ever could be. God is the one who is all-powerful, who makes everything and sets everything in motion. That is the First Person of God, and what an important part that is!

Second, God came to us in the human form of Jesus. This is important because Jesus is like us and knows us. Jesus knows how wonderful it can be sometimes—and how sad it is other times—to be a human being. Jesus was human in all the ways we are. But Jesus also was divine, meaning he was God's chosen one. He was born, he lived, he died on the cross, and then he rose to life again on Easter. Jesus is our Savior, because he shows us the victory over sin and death that God wants us to know. So the Savior is also a very important person of God.

The third person of God is the Holy Spirit, which came in a special way after Jesus was no longer living in the world. The Holy Spirit is the part of God that sustains us. "Sustain" means giving us strength and courage and guidance from day to day so that we know and do what is right. When we pray about something and then feel an answer about that prayer come to us, we know that the Holy Spirit is helping us to understand what God wants us to know. This person of God—like the Creator and the Savior—is also very important.

Christians have designed or built many things to remind them of these three persons of God. You see three circles or triangles on the cloths at the front of our church. As you come up the sidewalk to enter our building, you see that the part over the doorways is divided into three sections. These also are reminders to us of the three persons of God.

I hope you will remember what God the Creator, God the Savior, and God the Sustainer all mean to us. And I hope that three-leafed clovers and all the other symbols of three around us will remind you of each of these important ways that God comes to us and loves us.

---

30 · As a Father

SCRIPTURE LESSON: *1 Samuel 3:1—"Now the boy Samuel was ministering . . . under Eli."*
CONCEPT: *One of the best ways to understand God is as the most loving of parents. When children do not have a father or mother present in their daily lives, they look to someone else to fill that important role.*

Today is Father's Day. This is a national holiday, not a church holiday, but we want to talk about it because it is such an important idea for us. It is important because Jesus taught that God is the most loving parent ever, and understanding that is one of the best ways for us truly to know God.

Last month there was a special holiday for mothers, and today is a holiday to emphasize how important fathers are. That is wonderful. Dads who love their kids are very special people, and I am glad for this day when we take extra time to say thanks to them.

Tell me some examples of loving things that fathers may do with their children. . . . Reading to them. . . . Holding them when they are extra sad or worried, or just any time. . . . Helping them to learn what is right. . . . Earning money to take care of them. . . . Playing ball and going places with them. . . . Those are all wonderful examples! Thank you.

Not every child gets to be with his or her father all the time. Some children see their fathers only once in a while. Other children, for many different reasons, do not ever get to see their fathers. In those cases, children almost always find someone else that they can be with or think of as a father. Do any of you have a special man in your life with whom you get to do some of those things we mentioned? . . . Okay, Jamie, tell me about your uncle. . . . He sounds like a wonderful man! . . . Thank you, Craig, I am glad for your grandfather, too. . . . Thank you, Jeremy. Yes, your family friend must be a very special man.

I have learned that every child needs both a special woman and a special man to look up to. Usually, parents get to be those important people. When that is not possible, we find someone else to be that special person.

In the Bible we learn about a boy named Samuel, who could not grow up near to his own father, so he became like a son to a wonderful man named Eli. Through Eli, Samuel learned much about God that would help him through all of his life.

Remember that God loves us like the most wonderful father or mother ever! Jesus taught us that, and it is a very important lesson. I am glad for the loving mothers and the fathers who get to be with their children to care about them and to teach them what is important.

On this Father's Day, I am thinking about those parents, but I am also thinking about other men who are there for children whose own fathers cannot be with them. Thank you, God, for these special men! Thank you for how much they help to show us your love for all children.

31 · Prayer versus Prayer

SCRIPTURE LESSON: *Hebrews 10:36—"For you need endurance, so that when you have done the will of God, you may receive what was promised."*

CONCEPT: *Prayer is very important. Answers to prayers are not always given immediately as "yes" or "no," but may come only over a period of time.*

Baseball season is in full swing now. Some of you play on a league team, and some of you play in your neighborhood. And some of you like to watch games at the ballpark or on television. I like to do that too!

The other day I was watching a game on television, and as a certain player came up to bat the announcer said that this would be his first time ever to bat in the major leagues. I noticed that before this batter came up to the plate, he paused and seemed to be praying. Then he stepped up for his turn at bat.

This was a good thing to do. The Bible tells us that we should pray about all things and know that God is always with us and hears us. I began to wonder, though, if that prayer was going to be answered with a base hit.

What do you think? Do you think that a batter will get a hit if he or she prays before batting? . . . What, Ashley? Have you done that, too? Yes, many of us have prayed before batting, or before doing something important. . . . Yes, Amber, I agree with you. God would not help a batter get a base hit just because he or she had prayed for it, but praying would certainly help the batter to do his or her best .

Now I have another question, and it may be a more difficult one. What do you think happens if the batter prays to get a hit, but the pitcher prays for the batter to strike out? Suppose each prays as sincerely as the other. What do you believe will happen? . . . That is not an easy question, and one we really cannot answer, can we?

I have wondered about questions like these for a long time. I have always believed that God wants to answer our prayers. Yet I know that often people pray at the same time for things that are the opposite of one another. A group of children may pray for a sunny day for their picnic on the same day that the farmers pray for rain for their crops. The children have looked forward to their picnic, so that is a good request. The farmers need rain to help them grow food for children who want to have picnics, so that is a good request, too.

There are many situations when only one thing can happen at a time, but when more than one thing would have been good to have happened. God wants to answer our prayers, and yet not every prayer can be answered at any one time.

I told you I have been wondering about questions like these for a long time, and I thank you for your ideas. You are helping me to understand that although we want our prayers to be answered right away, maybe God answers most prayers over a long period of time.

As we pray—and do our best—and pray some more—and do our best some more—slowly, over a long time, as we learn and grow, we can see more and more how God is with us and always has been with us. We can see how God answers prayers over time in our lives. That is what God wants for us, because God cares about us so much.

. . . What, R.G.? What happened after I saw the batter pray? Well, he hit the ball very hard, but the center fielder caught it for an out.

That batter did well, but he still made an out. If he continues to try hard and play his best and pray for God to be with him whenever he plays—I am sure that he will play very well.

32 · Paint Your Wagon—Again

SCRIPTURE LESSON: *2 Timothy 1:5—" . . . a faith that lived first in your grandmother Lois and your mother Eunice and now, I am sure, lives in you."*

OBJECT NEEDED: *Something of great personal value that spans generations*

CONCEPT: *The story of God's love in Christ is so wonderful that just as we learned it from those older than ourselves, we now want to teach it to those younger.*

Today I am going to show you something that is very, very special to me. . . . Here it is! Yes, it is a red wagon, just big enough for a child to sit in. Two can sit in it together if they squeeze in just right.

Would anyone like to sit in the wagon right now? . . . Good, Katie, and Allyson, you want to get in, too? Okay . . . there. See how wonderful this wagon is! I can pull Katie and Allyson right along with me, and we can go to the park or to the store or wherever we want to go. Does anyone else have a wagon like this? . . . Breck and Grier, you do?

There are many wagons like this one—but this one is special to me because my parents bought it for me when I was very young. I rode in it and played with it from the time that I was two or three until I was about seven or eight. Then I got too big for it, so it was put away for a long, long time.

A few years ago, when my own boys were little, my father got this same wagon out from where it had been kept, because he wanted my children to have it. At first we did not think they would be able to play in it because it was so rusty and broken from sitting in the garage all those years. But my father sanded off the rust and then painted the wagon with the bright red paint you see. Then he oiled all the wheels and got a new wheel to replace one that had been broken. He tightened and polished— and then it was ready! And Nevin and Caleb both used it for a long time while they were growing up.

During those years that Nevin and Caleb were little, my father—their grandfather—died. We were all very sad and missed him very much. But every time we looked at the little red wagon we felt a little bit better. It reminded us of the wonderful things my father had done.

Finally, Nevin and Caleb also were too big for the wagon, and we put it away again. This time I was very careful to put it in a place where it would stay dry and safe. After a few more years, something wonderful happened to us. Sara came into our family. Soon she also was just the right size for the wagon.

Now it makes me happy again to see Sara play with the wagon. Even though she never got to meet her Grandpa Steindam, I can feel that he is with her and loves her when I see her in the wagon that he bought for me when I was little and then fixed to be like new for his grandchildren. Now, ten years later, it is being used once more, and I am very glad.

At our church we call today Christian Education Sunday. We say "thank you" today to all the people who have helped to teach others the stories of Jesus and of God's love during this past year. We are thankful for our teachers and youth workers. We are thankful also for parents and grandparents and aunts and uncles and other special friends—for everyone who helps to pass on the stories of God's love.

God's love is the most wonderful gift we have. And we want to take care of that gift and use it and make it available to those who will live in the future. Just as this wagon means more and more to me as it is used by my children, it also means more to know that God's love has been passed on from their grandparents and now from their parents to them. It means so much to know that they are now learning the very same stories that I learned long ago when I was their age.

I am glad for this red wagon and for what it helps me to remember. I am glad for you and for special gifts that your grandparents and parents have shared with you. Most of all, I am glad for the story of our faith in the God who loves us, because that is the greatest gift of all.

33 · Old Friends

SCRIPTURE LESSON: *Acts 1:21–22—"So one of [those] who have accompanied us during all the time . . . must become a witness."*

OBJECT NEEDED: *A doll, blanket, or other item that is old and worn*

CONCEPT: *Often we need the security of being with someone—or something— that we have known for a long time.*

Mrs. Marsh, who has been a member of our church for a long time, showed me something recently. It is so special to her that I asked her if I could show it to you today. . . . It is this doll.

Can you tell that this doll is very old? . . . Yes, it is worn down in some places, and it is missing parts of its hair and clothing. This doll was Mrs. Marsh's favorite when she was growing up—and that was more than seventy years ago! All the years since then, Mrs. Marsh has saved this doll. She has taken care of it as well as possible, but even so it has worn out in some ways and does not look as nice as new dolls do.

Why do you think she kept this doll all these years? Why hasn't she thrown it out and bought a new one that looks nicer and that can talk and do all the other things that dolls today can do? . . . Yes, Ingrid, . . . and yes, Geoffrey, those answers are very good. It is because this doll is the most special one in the world to Mrs. Marsh. It is the doll she had during

---

happy days and sad ones, the one that was with her on nights when she couldn't sleep, and the one she could tell secrets to that she couldn't tell anyone else. It is the doll that was with her as she was growing up, and no other doll could take its place.

Do any of you have a special doll or stuffed animal or blanket that you have had for a long time? . . . Yes? . . . Tell me about them . . . .

Just about all of you have something that is like a very special friend to you, and that you would never trade for anything. Tyler, it sounds as though you would not give up your blanket for a new one, even though it is beginning to come apart! And the same is true for the rest of you with your special things.

All of us, whether we are young children like you or adults like Mrs. Marsh, sometimes need a special friend to help us feel good. A special friend can help us feel more brave about something, or help us feel happier when we are sad. Certain things that we have known for a long time, like dolls or blankets or favorite books, can be this kind of friend for us.

Most wonderful of all are the people who have been special to us for a long time. Our parents, our grandparents, our teachers, and our friends all help us feel good about ourselves in the ways that God wants us to. They help us do the things that are most important for us to do.

I am so glad for the special friends God gives us. I am glad for things like a worn-out blanket or an old doll or teddy bear that we have held and hugged on many, many days. I am even more glad for the special people who love us and have been with us for a long time.

34 · Hibernation Anticipation

SCRIPTURE LESSON: *Exodus 3:10—"So come, I will send you to Pharaoh to bring my people, the Israelites, out of Egypt."*

OBJECT NEEDED: *A clump of brown grass, or something else that appears lifeless*

CONCEPT: *Some parts of the natural world go into a quiet period, then spring to new life when God calls. The same can be so of people.*

We have gone a long time without rain this summer, haven't we? Does anyone know how long it has been? . . . Yes, Peter, you are right. It has been about two weeks since any rain fell, and it has been a dry summer overall.

When there is no rain for a long time, many things do not look as nice as they usually do. Our lawns, especially, show the effects of the dry weather. . . . Yes, Sarah, they look brown and dead, don't they? I brought in a little clump of grass from our side yard. It looks dead, doesn't it?

I have been reading about grass and about what happens to it during a dry spell like this, and I have learned some remarkable things. I learned that this grass, even though it looks dry and brown, is not really dead. Because of our dry weather, the grass has become dormant. That means it has gone into a state of protecting itself and just being quiet for a while. During this time the grass does not grow. No one has to mow the lawn these days! No, the grass is not growing, but it is waiting. Down in the ground, the roots are still alive. And someday soon, when rain does fall, we will all be amazed by the new, green grass that will sprout from the roots underneath. What looks dead really isn't dead. It is just waiting until the right time.

Some animals get through the winter by doing something similar. They hibernate. They go into such a quiet, deep sleep that it seems as if they are dead, but they aren't! They are just waiting for spring, when they will be ready to do all the things they like to do once again. They will spring back to life with the warmer weather.

People do not hibernate the way animals do, and we do not become dormant like the grass. But we are like them in some ways. All of us have busy and exciting times in our lives. But we also have quieter times. My son, Caleb, had been a busy, outgoing boy where we used to live. Then we moved here, and he had to leave his friends and the places he had known so well. For a while after we moved, Caleb was very quiet and not so sure about things. But after a while it was as if he had awakened again, and he became more outgoing and active with new friends and new places that he liked.

All of us have times when we are quiet, when we are just waiting, and that is fine. When the time is right, God calls us again to be more active and to do new things.

This was true even for one of the great people of the Bible. Moses went through a very quiet time in his life. And then one day God called him and said, "I need you to go back to Egypt and to help my people there!" And Moses surely changed! At first he was not sure, but after he knew God had called him he became brave and outgoing in the ways God showed.

Right now this grass is in a very important state. It is waiting and ready for that time when God's rain will call it to something new. The same may be true for many of us right now, or perhaps it has been in the past or will be in the future. Sometimes we all need to be quiet for a while, just as this grass is right now. When we know that God is calling us, though, we go from that quieter time to something new, and know that we will be able to do whatever it is that God will show us.

35 · Being a Helper

SCRIPTURE LESSON: *Jeremiah 1:7—"Do not say I am only a [child]."*
OBJECTS NEEDED: *A number of small items that were purchased at a store*
CONCEPT: *Even at a very young age, children can be helpful.*

I have been thinking about something that happened this week. Maybe you can help me with my thinking. I am trying to figure out if my little girl, Sara, was a helper to me.

I had to go to the store across the street to get some things, and I took Sara with me. Because of the traffic, I carried Sara into the store, and then I carried her out of the store. When we left, not only did I have to carry her, but also the things that I had bought.

Let me show you some of those things. . . . A hat . . . a loaf of bread . . . a newspaper . . . a gallon of milk . . . and a little bag of school supplies. Here is what I have been trying to figure out. Sara carried some of the things that we had bought. But, I carried Sara while she carried them. So my question is this: Was Sara a helper or not in that situation? . . . Okay, Michael says that she was a helper to me, and I think that he is right. Sara sat on my arm, and that still left me with two hands, plus her

82

two hands for carrying things. She held the little bag of school supplies in one hand and the loaf of bread in the other, and she even wore the new hat that I had bought. So even though I had to carry Sara, she did help because she was able to hold things for me. I really needed extra hands right then, and she was able to offer hers for the job we had to do together.

Tomorrow is a holiday that may sound a little bit funny to some of you. It is called Labor Day, and it is a holiday with a special meaning. . . . Yes, Brian, you are right. You just started school last week, and you get tomorrow off as a holiday! Labor is another name for work. On Labor Day we give thanks for the work that each of us is able to do, and we give thanks for the work that others do, too, because only by living and working together can we have all the things that we enjoy so much.

Usually when we talk about work, we mean the jobs that adults or older teens have, but I want us to remember that every one of us can do important work whenever we try to help someone. Tell me about some jobs that you do to help others . . . . Pulling weeds or raking leaves . . . setting or clearing the dinner table . . . helping your teacher pass out papers to the class. . . . Those are all wonderful ways of helping others!

Even though you do not have the kind of job that means you must go someplace to work each day, this holiday called Labor Day is still for you. It is for you because you are helpers and because you learn to do more things every day.

I told you that at first I was not sure if Sara was a helper on our trip home from the store. Probably part of the reason I was not sure is that she is little, and sometimes we think that small children cannot do helpful jobs. But I was wrong. She really was a helper. I needed her extra hands and she offered them!

Just as Sara was helpful, I know that you are helpful too, in many different ways every day. I am so glad that God has made you the way that you are! I am glad that you want to learn and want to help others however you can. Tomorrow, as you celebrate Labor Day, I want you to think about all the ways that you are helpful to others, and to know how glad you make us.

36 · Moon over My Amazement

SCRIPTURE LESSON: *Psalm 8:3—"When I look at your heavens, the work of your fingers, the moon . . ."*
OBJECTS NEEDED: *Simple drawings of the moon in its different phases and a calendar that lists the phases*
CONCEPT: *The exact changes of the moon are one of the many things that show the greatness of God.*

I have some drawings to show you. I am not especially good at drawing, but I think you will be able to tell what I had in mind as I did these. . . . Here is the first one. . . . It looks like a circle . . . and now . . . half a circle . . . and look at these. . . . Yes, now you know! You are right, Amber, these are drawings of the moon and of the changes that it goes through every month.

The word "month" was made up because it sounds like the word "moon." Month . . . moon. It takes twenty-nine and one-half days—just about one month—for the moon to go through all of its phases, from full . . . back to full again.

Actually, the moon does not change. It does not really get bigger or smaller during the month. It only looks that way to us because of the shadow that is on it. Depending on where the moon is in relation to the earth and the sun, we can see only certain portions of it throughout the cycle that it makes each month.

So the moon goes through all of these phases, always in the same order, always in the same amount of time. These things are so exact that they can be predicted long in advance. I have a calendar here that tells the times for the phases of the moon a whole year in advance. This is amazing to me—to be so exact a full year ahead!

And yet, this is only a small amount of time compared to what can be predicted. Those who understand the moon and the timing of its changes can figure out years and years in advance the exact dates for each of the changes in the moon.

There are many things that tell me how great God is—and this is one of the most wonderful of all. God set the moon into motion with such precision! The moon gives light at night through what it reflects from the sun. It makes tides move on the great seas and oceans of the world. It affects how our crops grow. Most of all, the moon is like a special friend that is with us in the night. It is friendly and reliable, and many poems and songs and stories have been written about it.

The book of the Bible called Psalms contains many verses that praise God. One of my favorites tells how everything that we see in the sky—including the moon—shows us how great God is. Yes, God made all these wonders that are set in the sky with such exact movements. And the Psalm says that very same God—who is so great and so wonderful—cares about you and me most of all. Of all that God has made, we are the most wonderful, for we have been made in God's own image.

There is so much that causes me to want to praise and thank the God who loves me. I look at the moon and I feel as though It Is a friend I can count on. I think about how dependable and exact It Is In its twenty-nine and one-half day cycle. I look at that great, beautiful moon, and I think about how the God who made that also made me, and loves me and cares about me most of all.

God is so wonderful and God is so great. Like the person who wrote the Psalm, we want to praise God—in our worship and in our lives every day!

37 · Not a Ruth-less Situation

SCRIPTURE LESSON: *Ruth 4:15*—*" . . . for your daughter-in-law who loves you, who is more to you than seven sons. "*

CONCEPT: *God is with any family where there is love and caring, blessing them and bringing even more good to them.*

I remember very clearly something that I talked about with my friends a long, long time ago. I was about nine years old at the time—the age that some of you are now. A friend of mine named Paul had begun to tell the rest of us about his new stepmother. His father had just gotten married, and his new wife was now Paul's new mother, or stepmother, as some people say.

Well, did we ever feel sorry for him! He had barely started to tell us about her when we started telling him how sad we were for him that he now had to live with a stepmother. We all were talking so much that Paul could hardly get another word into the conversation! He kept trying, though, and finally we did stop talking and listen long enough for him to tell us that we shouldn't feel sorry for him! He had wanted to tell us about how wonderful his new mother—or stepmother—was!

Well, we just couldn't believe it. We were sure we knew all about stepmothers and that they were always mean. Do you know what made us think that way? Why do you think we believed that stepmothers were always cruel? . . . Yes, Abby, that is exactly right. In many fairy tales there are bad stepmothers.

So we were all sure we knew the truth. But Paul said no, we didn't know the truth. And then he told us about all the caring things that his new mother did for him and his sister, and of how much she loved them and how wonderful it was to have her living in their home with them. And do you know what? Later, I got to meet Paul's new mother, and everything he had told us was true! She did love them very much and was kind and fun to be with, and I could understand why Paul had wanted to tell us all about her.

86

Yes, it is true that some stepmothers or stepfathers do not turn out to be good parents. But most times they are wonderful parents, just as God wants them to be. Almost all parents do try their best. They love their children and try to help them to grow up to be all that God has made possible for them to be.

There is beautiful story in the Bible about a woman named Ruth, who is married to the son of a woman named Naomi. Therefore Ruth is Naomi's daughter-in-law. In a way, she is like a stepdaughter to Naomi. The lesson of the story is that she loves Naomi just as much as if she were her daughter. Wonderful things happen to them because God's love is with them as they are a family together.

Many of you here today live with the people who are your parents by birth, and they love and care for you in many good ways. God's love is with you, and good things happen because of that. Others of you live with one parent or perhaps even two who have become your parents in some way since you were born. These persons love you very much and care for you, and God's love is there. So much good can happen because of that, just as my friend Paul wanted us to know this was happening for his family.

People can come to be a family in many different ways. A family does not have to be one certain way or have a certain number of people in it. What matters is that the people love each other and care for each other—and then we know God's love is there, too.

My friend Paul taught me a very important lesson. He let me see how loving and how wonderful his stepmother was to him. He helped me to see how wonderful it is to be in any family where there is love. I am glad for each one of you and for each family that loves you. I know that God will be with your families and that more good will continue to come to you because of that love.

38 · God's Handiwork

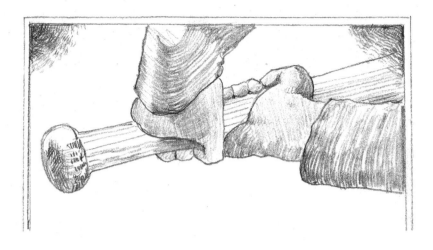

SCRIPTURE LESSON: *Lamentations 3:41—"Let us lift up our hearts as well as our hands."*
CONCEPT: *Our hands, with their opposable thumbs, are a gift showing God's greatness and love in our lives.*

I am going to show you one of the most amazing actions in the world. Some people would even call it a miracle! Watch. . . . Did you see that? . . . Maybe I should do it again. . . . Oh, that is such a wonderful thing to do!

. . . Yes, Taylor, all I did was move my thumb. First I stretched it out to the side, then I pressed it against my hand. . . . You can do that, too, and I am glad that you can. Some people might think this is not such a special action, since almost everyone can do it. But that is what makes this so wonderful and miraculous. Let me see how many of you can do this. . . . Yes, you all can!

Scientists tell us that we have opposable thumbs, and that this is one of the most important things about us humans. "Opposable" sounds like "opposite," doesn't it? This means that our thumbs bend in the opposite way from our fingers, so that the fingers and the thumb can work together to help us do things that we otherwise couldn't.

Now that summertime is here, many of us are doing things that we don't do the rest of the year. Many of these things require you to use your thumbs in special ways.

What are some things you are doing this summer? . . . Playing baseball. Yes, we need our thumbs to grip the ball or the bat, or to squeeze the glove when we catch the ball. . . . Swimming does not sound at first like something that we need our thumbs for, but they help us to swim better because they cut the water and pull us through it better and faster. . . . Reading also doesn't sound like something that needs a thumb, but we use our thumbs when we hold a book and turn the pages. . . . Playing the piano is another good example. The thumbs have very important jobs to do in playing the piano. . . . Yes, drawing or writing are things that we use our thumbs for. Without a thumb we could not get a perfect grip on our pencil or crayon or paintbrush.

There are so many things to do! And when we do good things with our hands and use our amazing thumbs, we make God very happy! This is because God has given us this wonderful gift. Now we give a gift back to God when we use our hands and thumbs for good things. We use our thumbs without even thinking about them. But today and through the busy, happy days of summer, please think about what a wonderful gift they are. Every now and then, pause for a moment and look at your thumbs, and think about the God who gave them to you and how much that God loves you. Then get busy using them again, and as you do good things, think about how happy you are making God.

39 · When We Need Reminding

SCRIPTURE LESSON: *Luke 15:31—"You are always with me, and everything that I have is yours."*
OBJECT NEEDED: *The poem below*
CONCEPT: *Nearly everyone becomes bored at some time, but the seasons and schedules we follow help us to appreciate and enjoy all that God gives to us.*

It's getting late in the summer now, isn't it? I remember when school ended for the year in June, and that seems like a very long time ago now. Does it seem that way to you, too? . . .

When I was growing up I couldn't wait for school to be out. I had so many things planned. But then, by the middle of August, I would begin to wonder what I could do. Sometimes I was even bored with so much time, because I couldn't think of enough things to do. . . . Bennett, do you feel that way sometimes? . . . Yes, you do, and others seem to feel the same.

A boy who is very special to me wrote a poem about this. I like the poem so much that I have memorized it and I want to say it to you. The poem is called "What'll We Do?" and it goes like this:

> *What'll we do? What'll we do?*
> *I don't know. How about you?*
>
> *Let's be a zoo!*
> *I'll be a kangaroo!*
> *Let's be a zoo!*
> *You can be an animal, too!*
> *But we can't be a zoo?*
> *Oh, boo, hoo, hoo, hoo!*
> *We're just a bunch of kids*
> *With nothing to do!*

What'll we do? What'll we do?
  I don't know. How about you?

Let's be a band!
  I'll be a drummer!
  Let's be a band!
You can be the violin strummer!
  But we can't be a band?
  Oh, what a bummer!
  We're just a bunch of kids
  Doing nothing in the summer!

What'll we do? What'll we do?
  I don't know. How about you?" *

Do you like that poem? . . . Yes, I do, too! It says how we all feel sometimes, especially in the last days of summer.

There is only one week left until school will start. I remember that I always would say that I didn't want school to start, but on the inside I really did. Summer is such a great time! But then it is good to go on to other things when summer is over.

What are some of the things that you have done during this summer vacation? Aaron has enjoyed going to the pool. . . . Jordan had fun on a family trip. . . . Kyle says he had fun just being at home. I am glad for all the things you have done. There have been many happy and good things in the summer, but school will bring many more good things to us.

Every day, no matter what the time of year, can be a special day because of what God makes possible for us. If every day were just the same, we would soon get bored. But that is not how God has made our lives. We have times to be at church, times to be at school, times to be at home, and times to be away somewhere else. I am glad for all the different times of our lives. They help us to stay excited about living, and to know how much God loves us.

Knowing that there are just eight more days before school starts helps us want to make the most of every one of those days. And then, when school starts next week, we know that we will be ready for that important and new time of our lives. Each new part of our lives helps us to be ready to be our best and to do our best as we enjoy all that God gives to us every one of our days.

*Used by permission of Nevin Steindam.

91

40 · Growing Outside and Inside

SCRIPTURE LESSON: *Luke 2:52—"And Jesus increased in wisdom and in years, and in divine and human favor."*
OBJECT NEEDED: *A very small tree with roots attached and with the seed from which it sprouted still identifiable*
CONCEPT: *All of us grow in the ways the Bible says Jesus grew, in ways we can see on the outside and ways hidden on the inside.*

We have an oak tree in the front yard at my house, and a few months ago the seeds that this tree makes began to fall on the ground. These seeds are called acorns. There is an old saying about acorns that some of you may have heard. The saying is "Great oaks from little acorns grow." That means that the oak tree, which is one of the greatest and grandest of all trees, grows from just a tiny acorn. The lesson of that saying is that some of the biggest and most important things begin in very small or simple ways.

At our house we also have squirrels, and they like to eat the acorns. They do not eat all of the acorns right away, though. They want to save some for later, and they do this by burying them in the ground. This is part of God's plan for new trees to grow, because some of the acorns that the squirrels bury for later begin to sprout from the ground as new trees.

I pulled out one of these little trees to show you this morning, and I was careful to pull out everything that is attached to it. I can see some important things. The first thing is that a little bit of the acorn shell is still here. Do you see it, Katie? . . . Yes, it was just below the ground. This is where everything started to grow to become this tree. The second thing I notice is how long the roots of this tree are. Look, they are as long as the tree that we can see above the ground is! That is very important, and I want us to think about it.

The Bible tells us that we grow in different ways. We grow on the outside, getting taller, just as this tree is growing above the ground where we can see it. But we also grow in ways hidden inside, as we learn more things and as we become more caring about other people, just as this tree is growing these roots down in the ground, where they are hidden.

Jesus was once a child, like each of you, and he grew in all the ways that you are growing. Jesus grew taller on the outside, but he also grew in what he learned and felt on the inside. The Bible tells us something else about the kind of growing Jesus did. It says he grew in how he got along with other people, and he also grew in knowing God's love and closeness.

All the ways that we grow are important. . . . What, Allyson? . . . Yes, your baby sister, Natalie, is growing in many ways right now, isn't she? And you are growing in many ways now, too. I am glad for all the ways that we grow, from the time when we are babies to the time when we are children, then teenagers, then adults. I am glad for the growing that we can see, like the growing of this part of the tree that is above the ground. But I am just as glad for the growing that is taking place where it is hidden from our eyes, just as these roots are hidden under the ground. I am glad for the ways we can grow in getting along with people, and for the ways we grow in knowing how much God loves us and is with us.

I am going to plant this little tree in a place where it will have room to grow great and tall, where it will have room to spread its branches above the ground and its roots below the ground, because that is the kind of growing God wants us all to do.

41 · Rocketed by Dreams

SCRIPTURE LESSON: John 14:12—"Very truly, I tell you, the one who
   believes in me . . . will do greater works than these."
OBJECT NEEDED: An out-of-date science book
CONCEPT: God continues to reveal new things to those who have faith,
   who dare to dream and discover.

Last week I was going through some boxes of things that I have had
since I was a little boy. One of the things I found was this old book that was
published back in 1959. It is called *Rockets into Space*, and it tells about all
the things that could happen as we try to explore outer space. I want to
read the final sentence of this book to you. It says, "Who knows? Someday, someone may even go to the moon!"

Well, as I read that I smiled. I smiled because I thought about how
people back then were dreaming that maybe someone would go to the
moon someday. Why do you think I would smile about that sentence in
this book? . . . Yes, Valerie, you are right. I smiled because now many
people have gone to the moon! Our first astronaut landed and walked
there a long time ago. . . . Yes, David, his name was Neil Armstrong, and
many others have been on the moon since then, too.

So many things have happened, so many big changes have taken place since I was a little boy that sometimes I smile when I think of them. When I read a book like this one, I smile because it seems out-of-date or behind what has happened in our world since then. When I was a boy we dreamed about many things that have happened in our world since then.

But even though I smile about how much the people who wrote this book did not yet know, the dreams they talked about in this book were important, because they helped those things to one day happen! Great things begin to happen when someone believes that they can. When people dream about something, and think and think about it, they can find ways to make it happen. The authors of this book believed that someday someone might go to the moon. Believing that it could happen was a very important part of making it happen.

Many more good things will happen in this world. I will see some of them, and you will see even more of them. Maybe some of you will discover or invent new things. There are diseases that don't have a cure today, but will someday. There are hungry people with not enough food today, but with better ways to grow food and to share our food everyone will have enough someday. There will be many more discoveries and inventions that will help us to travel and communicate and care in greater and greater ways.

. . . What, Kathy? . . . What I said about diseases made you think about AIDS? . . . Yes, that is a very sad disease. . . . I am glad to hear that you have been talking about it at your school and here at church school. You are right. We need to help people who have AIDS, but we do not need to be afraid of them, and, yes, someday someone will find a cure for this disease. It is even possible that someone here will help to find that cure! That will be wonderful and will make God very happy!

God has made us so that we are able to think and to discover new things. When we believe that something can happen, when we dream about it and then go to work on it, we can bring about new ideas and inventions.

This book reminds me of how much good has happened since I was your age. I am glad for people who dreamed and believed and helped to make these things happen. And I am glad for each one of you, and for the ways God has made you, so that you may make new inventions or discoveries to help all the people of the world.

42 · Time To Get to It!

SCRIPTURE LESSON: *Isaiah 6:8—"Here am I; send me!"*
OBJECTS NEEDED: *Small paper circles with the letters TUIT printed on them*
CONCEPT: *When Gods calls us, it is the time to do what we know we are called to do.*

I am going to give each of you something very important. This object that I am handing out will be very helpful to you. . . . Here you are, Kyle, and Aaron . . . and everyone else.

Does everyone have one now? . . . Great! Can you see what these are? . . . Yes, Tyler, they have a funny-looking word on them, don't they? Each one of these is a "Round TUIT," and as far as I can tell, these are extremely important in helping people to do things. This is true for adults, and it is also true for children.

So many times I hear people say that they will do something just as soon as they get one of these. For example, just yesterday I heard someone say, "When I get a Round TUIT I am going to build a deck on my house." I heard a woman recently say, "When I get a Round TUIT I am going to go back to college." And the other day I heard a child say, "I'm going to be a good student and get better grades by studying harder. I just have to get a Round TUIT."

Have you ever heard people say things like that? . . . I have decided to do something about it. I have decided to help everyone by making some of these very important items that everyone seems to need, and I am beginning my work by giving one to each of you this morning. Now you will be able to do all sorts of things! What do you think of that? . . .

Yes, my idea is silly in one way, because this is not what people mean when they say those words. But, in another way, perhaps these words can help us. What we believe and decide in our own minds is what is most important. When we know that God is calling us to do something good, then we can say yes in answer to God and go ahead and do that good thing.

People have so many good ideas and plans. But we often put off doing anything about them. Perhaps we do not feel enough confidence in ourselves, or perhaps we feel lazy or too busy. But God wants us to go ahead and do those good things.

In one way this little circle of paper is silly, but in another way it is not. It reminds us of all the good things God wants us to do and that we *can* do when we say yes to God and believe in the abilities God has given us to do those things.

Now that we've all gotten a Round TUIT, what wonderful things we are going to do to serve our God!

43 · Broccoli Busters

SCRIPTURE LESSON: *Genesis 1:29—"God said, 'See, I have given you every plant . . . and every tree with seed in its fruit; you shall have them for food.' "*

OBJECT NEEDED: *A stalk of fresh broccoli*

CONCEPT: *God has given us many gifts of food, including a variety of each kind that we need.*

I have brought something in this grocery bag to show you today. . . . Do you know what this is? . . . Elyse knows! It is broccoli. I just bought this at the store, and tonight I will cook it and our family will eat it as part of our dinner.

How many of you like broccoli? . . . Hmmm, about half of you do. Tell me, is broccoli good for us? Is it a healthful food to eat? . . . Todd is right. It is very healthful. Broccoli has fiber and contains many of the vitamins that are most important in our diet.

As I learn about broccoli and about how good it is for us, I find myself worrying about what will happen to people who do not like it and do not eat it. Many children say they do not like the way broccoli tastes—as some of you said this morning—and I know that many adults also do not like it. Even a president of our country said he did not like to eat broccoli! I worry about this. What will happen to people who do not eat their broccoli? How can they possibly be healthy? . . . What did you say, Ryan? . . . Oh, I see. Even if people do not like broccoli, they can eat other things that are similar to broccoli in the kinds of nutrition they have.

Let's talk about that. What are some examples of other foods that have many of the same vitamins as broccoli? . . . Green beans . . . and peas . . . and other fruits or vegetables would be good. Many other vegetables that are green, as broccoli is, would be similar in nutrition.

Have any of you learned in school or at home about the food groups? Yes, different kinds of healthful foods belong in different groups or categories, and it is important for us to eat foods from each of these groups every day. Naturally, there are some foods that some people will not like as much, but that is all right as long as they are careful to eat other things from that same group of foods.

So, even if you do not like broccoli, you can still be healthy by eating other green vegetables. . . . What, Ed? . . . Oh, you don't like broccoli, but you must eat a little bit when it is put on your plate? . . . And, Ken, you say that you did not think you would like it, but after your parents made you try a little, you found out that it's not too bad? I am very glad to hear that!

God has made us and our world so wonderfully, with many different things that are good for us to eat. God wants us to be healthy, and so has given us a variety of foods that are important to our health. When we eat healthful things like broccoli or the many other good choices we have, we are taking good care of ourselves and are making God very happy.

44 · In the Key of Glee

SCRIPTURE LESSON: *Luke 22:19—"Do this in remembrance of me."*
OBJECTS NEEDED: *Colored key holders, which can be purchased in most hardware stores*
CONCEPT: *Some items or actions remind us of certain persons or experiences. Sharing communion is the most important and most wonderful of such actions.*

Can any of you tell what these are? . . . Yes, Bennett, they are little pieces of plastic. One is yellow and another is pink. In fact, there is one of almost every color.

It is difficult to know what these are or what they do by just looking at them. I did not know what they were, either, until I saw them being used. So, I will show you. . . . These are little coverings to slip over part of a key . . . like this. Many people buy these to help them tell their keys apart. If I know that this pink holder has the key for my office, then I can find it right away. People who use these just have to remember that the yellow one is for their car, and the blue one for their house, and so forth, and it saves them time.

Some of these have been used in another way, and that is what I want to tell you about this morning. I have a friend named Mr. Hephinger. . . . Yes, he is Chris and Danielle and Sara's grandfather. Mr. Hephinger has a sister, and he and his sister love each other very much. A few years ago, Mr. Hephinger's sister moved far away from him—all the way from Ohio to Florida. Even though she was happy about her new home, she knew that she would miss her brother and that he would miss her. Before she moved away, Mr. Hephinger's sister did something that surprised him. She bought some of these key holders, and she put them on his keys. Then she said to him, "Every time you look at one of these, I want you to think about me and remember how much I miss you and love you!" And so, he does! Mr. Hephinger tells me that he uses his keys many times every day, and each time he does, he remembers his sister and knows that even though he cannot see her, she is still with him because she loves him so much.

We are having communion at our church today. This is very special because people who believe that Jesus is Savior—no matter where they live in the world—are having communion today. I want to help you to understand the meaning of communion, and one of the ways I can tell you is that it is somewhat like these key holders and what they do for Mr. Hephinger. Jesus told his disciples that whenever they ate bread and drank from the cup of juice or wine, it should make them think about him. They were to be reminded of how much he loved them and was with them because of that love, even when they could no longer see him. Very much like Mr. Hephinger's keys, bread and grape juice were ordinary things for the disciples. They were sure to see and to use them almost every day. And so, whenever the disciples broke off a piece of bread from a loaf, or whenever they had a drink of grape juice or wine from a cup, they would remember Jesus. Then they would feel so much joy, because they would know that even though they could not see Jesus, he was still with them because he loved them so much.

Again today we are doing what Jesus asked us to do by taking these gifts he gave us and thinking about what they mean, just as Mr. Hephinger does with the special gifts his sister gave him.

Communion is a wonderful gift, and there is much to learn about it. I hope that this story of Mr. Hephinger's key holders, and of the ways they are happy reminders to him, will help us to understand a little bit more about the gift Jesus gave all of us in communion.

45 · Seeing What Matters

SCRIPTURE LESSON: *Matthew 15:18—"But what comes out of the mouth proceeds from the heart."*

OBJECT NEEDED: *Something the storyteller can point out about himself or herself that is different from what had been previously*

CONCEPT: *Outside appearances are not what is important about us. It is who we are on the inside that matters.*

Can anyone see what is different about me today? . . . What, Dawn? . . . That is right! I have not shaved today. I have not shaved since Friday, because I have decided to grow a beard.

I wonder if having a beard will make me different. What do you think? Will I be a different person than I am now when my beard is grown out? . . . Yes, I will *look* different, won't I? But will I *be* different? Will it make me a meaner person or a nicer person? . . . Karen says that I won't be any different in those ways. I will still be the same person, whether I have a beard or whether my face is shaved.

This is a lesson that Jesus thought very important to have us understand. He knew that it does not make any difference if a person wears an earring or not, or has long hair or short hair or no hair. He knew that what kind of clothes people choose to wear does not make a difference in whether or not they are kind.

The important things about people are the things that are known and felt on the inside. If a person is filled with love and kindness, that is what matters more than anything else.

All of us can choose how we want to dress or how we want to look. Those are personal choices, and each of us will agree with some choices and disagree with some choices that others make. Some things are considered to be in style one year and then out the next, as different looks come and go.

Once again, though, we remember what Jesus said, that the things on the outside of people are not what matter very much. What matters are the thoughts and the feelings that are on the inside of each person.

In the coming weeks, as my beard grows, I believe you will see that I am the same person with my beard as I have been without one. I believe that we will all understand that Jesus was right: it is not how we look on the outside, but who we are on the inside, that matters most of all.

46 · Ready for Anything!

SCRIPTURE LESSON: *Ephesians 6:13—"Therefore take up the whole armor of God, so that you may be able to withstand . . ."*

OBJECT NEEDED: *An infant's diaper bag, filled with the things that may be needed to care for a baby*

CONCEPT: *Just as we must be prepared for whatever may happen or be needed in caring for a baby, we must also be prepared for all things in our own lives. That is why we learn so many lessons about many different parts of God's Word.*

Today I am helping a friend by taking care of her baby for the morning. I have brought this bag along to help me do a good job. It has all sorts of things in it that help me take care of her.

Let's see what is in here. . . . First, here is her favorite blanket. Can you tell me why I would keep that in here? . . . Yes, Craig, it keeps her warm if the weather gets cooler, and it makes her happy because it is her favorite. Here are more things that keep her happy . . . some of her little toys to hold or look at or listen to. . . . Here are some bottles . . . one has apple juice and the other has milk . . . and here are little packs of crackers in case she gets hungry. . . . Of course, we must have a couple diapers. . . . What? . . . Yes, Christopher—just in case she has to poop! We might as well be honest about that! Even though many different things are in this bag, people usually refer to it as a diaper bag because those are the most important things in here!

We have said that each thing has a good reason for being in here. And each one of them may be necessary to take care of the baby as we go through the morning. This bag helps me to be prepared for anything that may happen as I care for her.

Many things can happen to a baby, but even more things can happen or more things be needed as we grow bigger. That is why we want always to learn more about God's Word in the Bible. At home and at church school and at worship, we learn more and more of the things that the Bible teaches.

The Bible has so much in it! It teaches about all the different things that we may have to face or do in our lives. Sometimes we are happy, and sometimes things happen that make us feel sad. Sometimes we have to make a hard choice about something, and sometimes we need help in getting along better with someone. The Bible helps us to be prepared. It helps with all the kinds of things that we may have to think about or do as we grow up.

The Bible is not something that we can learn about all at once. That is why Sunday church school is held not just once, but every week. There are always more things to gain from the Bible, more to know about God's love for us, to help us to be prepared for the different things that may happen in our lives.

This diaper bag, with all the things in it, reminds me of how much is needed to take care of a baby. It also reminds me that as we grow up we need even more things in order to be able to take good care of ourselves and one another. I am glad for all that is in the Bible that helps us to know God's love and to be prepared for whatever may happen.

47 · A Most Familiar Face

SCRIPTURE LESSON: *1 Peter 1:8—"Although you have not seen him, you love him."*
OBJECTS NEEDED: *Several pictures of Jesus*
CONCEPT: *Although we have not seen Jesus face to face, we feel we know him as a friend.*

I have several pictures with me this morning. None of the pictures has a name on it, so I hope you will be able to help me figure out who these people are. Please take a look at this one . . . and this one . . . and this. . . .

What, Aaron? . . . You say that this is a picture of Jesus. . . . Okay, and Jordan says that this one also is Jesus. . . . And this one, too? You say that all of these are pictures of Jesus.

But take a moment and look at them again. In this picture the person has long hair, and here it is short. In this picture the person has a full beard, and in that one he has only part of a beard. Look what color his skin is in this one, compared to the others. And the faces look quite different from picture to picture.

. . . But, even so, you will not change your minds, will you? You still say that each of them is a picture of Jesus. How can you be so sure? . . . You say that you don't know how you know—you just do! That is a very good answer. Many people feel just as you do about this question.

There were no cameras at the time when Jesus lived, so we have no photographs of him. As far as we know no one painted any portraits of him, either. So we do not know what Jesus looked like, yet we all have an idea, a feeling of how he looked. And when we see a picture of him, we somehow know who it is.

Some of the artists who painted these pictures said that they felt God inspiring them—or directing them—to paint a picture of Jesus to look a certain way. Some have said they had a dream of how Jesus looked, or they prayed and felt that God answered the prayer by having them decide to paint Jesus in a certain way. When I think of these things, it helps me understand how we can recognize Jesus right away in these pictures. God helped each artist paint each picture, so God also helps us to see Jesus in each one.

There is a verse in the Bible that is very special to me. It says that even without seeing Jesus in person, we know him and love him just as much as we would if we had seen him and known him for a long time. Jesus lived long, long ago. But Jesus also lives with us now. Jesus lived with people far away from here. But Jesus is also a best friend for each of us.

Only God can make such a wonderful thing happen. Even though these pictures are different, you can tell that the person being pictured is Jesus. You recognize Jesus in these pictures because you first see him with the love in your heart.

48 · Free To Be Me

SCRIPTURE LESSON: *Psalm 33:22—"Let your steadfast love, O [God], be upon us, even as we hope in you."*
OBJECTS NEEDED: *Some colorful fall leaves*
CONCEPT: *It is fun to pretend to be someone or something else when we get into costume for Halloween. It is best of all, however, just to be ourselves.*

I have been collecting some of the most colorful and beautiful leaves. I am sure many of you also collect leaves at this time of year. Here are some of the ones I think are especially pretty. . . . Here is a brilliant red one . . . and an orange one . . . and one that is mostly yellow with orange sprinkles through it . . . and here is a brown one . . . . Yes, Sara, I think the brown ones are very pretty, and I am glad that you and Michael like to collect this kind, too.

During the spring and the summer the leaves are green. But then they turn different colors before they fall to the ground as the weather gets colder. We all think that the natural color for leaves is green, because they usually are green. I have been reading, though, that these fall colors are the true colors of the leaves. During the spring and summer there is chlorophyll in the leaves. Have you learned that word at school? Chlorophyll causes the deep green color that comes into the leaves and is so strong that it makes them look that color to us. But in the fall, the chlorophyll stops being made, and so the true colors, the natural colors of the leaves, come out. And most people believe that these are the prettiest colors of all.

This makes me think about what is so fun this week. It is Halloween week, and I know that many of you like to dress up and look like someone or something else. That is fun, and I am glad we all get to do that, but what is best of all is to be who we really are—as these leaves are doing right now. When we are who we truly are, we are the most beautiful and wonderful of all.

What will you pretend to be for Halloween? . . . Oh, those are all great ideas! Some of them are things I was when I was a child, and some of them are completely different! It is fun to pretend and to be something different. That is why Halloween is such a fun time. But when it is over it is best of all to be who we really are.

God loves us and made us the way we are. And so our hope and our happiness are found in God, just the way we are. I hope that as you look at the beautiful colors of the leaves this fall they will help you remember that what is most beautiful is the true and natural way that God has made you.

Please be safe and have fun on Halloween—and then afterward have the most fun of all by being you!

49 · Looking Up

SCRIPTURE LESSON: *Psalm 121:1*—*"I lift up my eyes to the hills— from where will my help come?"*

CONCEPT: *When we look upward, we tend to think more positively, to feel better, and to know that God is near. This is part of what worship leads us to do.*

This morning I want to talk with you about some important ideas. First of all, I want to talk about how we look and how we act when we are very sad. Chelsea, will you help me for a minute? I'd like you to stand here and show how you look when you are sad. . . .

Is everyone able to see Chelsea? She does look sad, doesn't she? Besides the sad look on her face, another thing that I notice is that she is looking down. Her head is down, and her shoulders and the rest of her body droop.

We do this very thing when we are sad. We look down, and we curve our bodies over in order to look down. Then, by doing this, we feel sadder still!

When we are looking down we do not breathe as deeply, so we don't get as much oxygen into our lungs. Also, when we slump over in this way, we feel more aches or pains. Finally, when we look down, we miss seeing many things. We do not notice much of what is happening around us.

A very important verse in the Bible says we should look up and know that God is with us. That does not mean that God is high up in the sky somewhere. But it does mean that the Bible writers knew that we feel better and can do more things in good ways when we are looking up.

Let's try this and see if it is true. What are some things you can see right now if you look up? . . . Very good, Connor. We see the cross and the windows and the ceiling. If we were outside right now, what might we see by looking up? . . . Clouds . . . birds . . . the sun and the sky . . . mountains . . . trees and tall buildings. What a wonderful list you have made! If it were nighttime and we looked up, we would see the stars or the moon! All these are things that help us feel good.

When we look up, other good things happen, too. We breathe more deeply and get more oxygen in our lungs. We have good posture and our bodies feel better. We feel more like walking or running or playing. All these things work together to help us know that God is with us, and they also help us know that God wants us to continue to do certain things.

Our church is built in such a way that when people come in here, they automatically look up. The windows and the cross and even the shape of the room cause our eyes to look up, and as we do that we feel better and we know that God is with us. That is an important part of worship, and I am glad that it happens here.

Sometimes sad things happen in our lives, and when they do, it is natural for us to want to look down. Then looking down can cause us to feel sadder still. Let's always remember, though, that God loves us and is with us even in the saddest of times. When we know this we look up and we see everything that God wants us to see. We breathe deeply and we move more freely. How glad I am that we can look up and find all the good things God wants us to see and do. How glad I am that looking up reminds us that God loves and is with us always!

50 · We Never Know

SCRIPTURE LESSON: *Philemon 11—"Formerly he was useless to you, but now he is indeed useful."*
OBJECT NEEDED: *A moldy piece of bread or cheese*
CONCEPT: *We often think that something (or someone) cannot be of any help to us, but we never know what God has in mind.*

Yesterday I opened our bread box to get some bread for a sandwich, and I noticed a small bag hidden at the back. It had just one piece of bread left in it when it was somehow pushed to the back corner. So, I took it out . . . and look at what had happened to it! . . . It had become covered with mold!

Yes, Cami, you are right! Yuck! It does not look at all nice! When we find something like this, what do we do with it? . . . Yes, we throw moldy bread away, don't we? We look at it and can tell right away that it would not be good to keep.

No matter how it looks, though, there is something very amazing and wonderful about mold like this. It has something in it that is very helpful. Mold, you see, is alive. It grows from the bread or cheese or whatever food has it. Back in the year 1928, a scientist named Sir Alexander Fleming discovered that something in mold was able to kill certain kinds of germs. It took him thirteen years of work, but he finally was able to get that important material out of the mold, and he called this new discovery penicillin. It was a very wonderful discovery. The new kind of medicine he discovered was called an antibiotic, and since then many other kinds of antibiotics have been made. The word "antibiotic" means that this kind of medicine kills germs that get into our bodies.

Devin, I know that you took an antibiotic when you were getting over your strep throat. Probably all of us have been given an antibiotic at some time to help us get well from some kind of sickness. This is so wonderful, and it is all thanks to the mold that we sometimes see growing on old food.

Many times we look at something and think that it is not good for anything. But perhaps it can do something very good. The same thing sometimes happens when we think about people. Someone may not look very able to do important or helpful things. Sometimes we even feel this way about ourselves. We may be feeling very sad, and when we are feeling that way we may think—we may even say—that we are not able to do anything good or helpful. I know that sometimes I feel this way. Everyone does sometimes. But God has made each of us in a very special way, and each of us can do many good things. We just need to be ready to discover those things and put them into action.

Sometimes when I am feeling sad, I think about the mold I have seen on some food, such as this piece of bread. Then I think about what a marvelous thing God had planned for that mold. Then I think to myself that if God had planned for mold to be used for something as important and as wonderful as penicillin and antibiotics, then surely God has many wonderful ways planned for me to be helpful, too!

51 · Apple-Eyeing Some Rules for Sharing

SCRIPTURE LESSON: *Philippians 4:10—"Indeed you were concerned for me, but had no opportunity to show it."*
OBJECTS NEEDED: *Two apples, one clearly larger than the other*
CONCEPT: *Even when we know that sharing is right and we want to share, we sometimes must search for the best way to do it.*

I have something to discuss with you this morning, and I want you to help me think about it. I want you to think of what you would do if this happened.

Kristen and Nicholas, would you stand beside me to help us? . . . Okay, let's pretend that Kristen has invited Nicholas over to her house and that they have been playing together for a while. Now they are both hungry and decide to get a snack. They look in the fruit bowl and see these two apples. . . . Yes, Isaac, you are right. One apple is big and the other is small, isn't it? That is the problem I want to discuss with you. I want you to think about how these two friends can share in the best way. . . . What do you think? . . .

Spencer, that is a good idea. It would be very kind of Kristen to give the big apple to Nicholas, since he is her visitor. . . .

Palmer has a very good idea, too. If one of them is much hungrier than the other one, and they can both agree about who is hungrier, then it would be good for that person to have the bigger apple. That would be fair. . . .

Denise has another idea. The most equal way of all would be to cut both apples in half, and for each friend to have half of the big one and half of the little one. The only problem is that they would need a sharp knife and a grown-up to cut the apples for them. I do like that idea, though. . . . What, Ian? That reminds you of a riddle? . . . What do you do if there are five people and four apples? . . . Make applesauce! Yes, that is a great answer. The only trouble is that applesauce takes time to make, and Nicholas and Kristen are hungry now!

What, Palmer? . . . You need to think about this a little more? . . . You are right, it is not an easy problem to solve, is it? There is not one sure way of sharing sometimes. I am very happy about all the good ideas you have come up with, though, because each of them could be the one that would be the kindest and best way to share at a time like this.

What I want you to remember from this talk together is that sometimes it is not easy to know how to share in the best way. Even when we want to share and know that it is the right thing to do, we may not be sure how to do so. But if we want to share, and if we think about it and work together, we can find a good way to do it. I know this is true because of all the good ideas you have just had in our talk about what to do if there is one big apple and one small one.

Sometimes finding the best way to share is something that our whole church must work together to do. We want to find ways to help others as much as possible, and even if it's not easy at first, we can find those ways if we keep thinking and working together on it.

I am so glad for the ways you want to share, and glad that together we can find the best way.

52 · Members of God's Bucket Brigade

SCRIPTURE LESSON: *Colossians 1:12*—" . . . *while joyfully giving thanks to [God], who has enabled you to share in the inheritance of the saints.*"
OBJECT NEEDED: *A bucket*
CONCEPT: *By working together we accomplish the most, and we work together best in a spirit of thankfulness.*

Whenever we hear the fire siren, we know that firefighters are racing to a fire with their trucks and other equipment to try to put it out. I am grateful for these people and for the equipment they have for fighting fires. Many years ago there were no fire trucks or some of the other equipment that we have today, but there still were fires that had to be battled. Do you know what they did in those days to put a fire out? People would form bucket brigades. They would make a long line between the fire and a well or a big tub of water, and one by one they would pass buckets of water down the line to the fire . . . Here, let's show how that worked. . . . Travis, you stand here . . . and then Emily . . . and so forth. The first person dips the bucket and passes it on, then grabs another bucket and does the same, and so on. The buckets head down the line, and the last person throws the water on the fire. That would have been very hard work, but everyone would have shared a wonderful feeling when the job was done and the fire was out.

. . . Yes, Jeremy, I saw that on the news, too! I am glad you thought of that. After the recent hurricane, when supplies were sent to people in need, the workers unloaded the supplies and passed them out in a line like this.

Also, when floodwaters were rising in another part of our country, people worked together to pile sandbags to hold the water back, and they made lines like this to pass the sandbags along to where they were needed.

People have learned that by working together they can do the most good. Firefighters in years past and emergency workers today have learned this. If everyone ran with only one armful of supplies or one bucket of water or one sandbag, they would not do nearly as much good as if they got into a line and worked in the way we have shown today. Even with all the new equipment that fire fighters and others have today, forming a line and working together often gets the job done in the best way.

When I think about people like firefighters or emergency workers, and about how hard they work and what dangerous jobs they do, I realize that they are able to do these jobs because they are thankful people. They know how much all of us have been given and helped, and how blessed all of us are, and out of their thankfulness they want to do whatever they can to help others have the blessings God wants us to have.

What I see and what I learn from these special people is that when we are thankful we are most brave and able to do the most good.

In a church that follows the teachings of Jesus, we are reminded of God's love and blessing every time we are together. In a way, we all become members of God's bucket brigade at our church, because here we get organized and work together so that God's people can have the blessings God wants them to have. That is why in this Thanksgiving season we have been collecting food to give to families who do not have enough to eat. People have passed this food along from farms and factories and from stores and homes, and from here it will be passed on to the people who need it most right now.

What a wonderful feeling it is to be part of a group of thankful people who are working together to get something good accomplished! That may be the best feeling there can be!

Thanks to all of you for the things you do and share, and for the ways that you help others to have the good gifts that we know God wants all people to have. Remember that when you are thankful to God and care about others, you become members of God's bucket brigade and help more of God's good gifts to go where God wants them to be.

Conclusion

An ancient Russian proverb says, "There are three ways in which to experience eternity in this world: to plant a tree, to have a child, and to write a book."

I completed work on this third of a trilogy of books of sermons for children fifteen years after I began work on the first. Yet I realize that I am in ways younger now than I was then, for in these intervening years I have been blessed to share in all three of the treasures identified in that proverb. I have planted trees; I have had children; and I have written these books for and about children, using the image of trees in the titles and contents of each.

In a town where I used to live, I knew a man who years earlier had served a term on the local school board. Whenever he was asked what his accomplishments were while he held office, he would cite only one: he had saved the big tree that sat on the playground of the elementary school from being cut down. And that majestic, giving tree stands there still, proudly announcing the seasons, inviting climbers, and providing shade to the children and grandchildren and great-grandchildren of those it first befriended eighty years ago.

There are cycles of such wonder in this life, in this world. Children enter our midst with joy and hope and energy for life. At first they need to get a boost in order to climb the tree that stands before them, but with assistance, they do so—and what glory they know as they do. They continue to stretch and to learn and to grow, until one day they experience a rite of passage, and they become the ones who offer that boost. Now they encourage and lift and teach the members of the generation seeking to climb after them. Such rites of passage do not occur without ceremony. Certain words are repeated from child to child. Important passages are quoted again and again. Particular books are perpetual favorites and are read and passed on beneath and within the limbs of those trees.

This ever-renewing cycle, this full embrace of eternity as known in the proverb, did not come about by chance, and it does not continue by chance. The God who out of love created all that is has also set before us the ways that the wondrous cycle may be continued, and has entrusted to us the responsibility for its continuance. And so we are now called to give a boost to the next generation as we say thank you to the generation who assisted us.

Trees and children and books are surely this world's most pure expressions of the eternal. Those who know this find ways to continue to be the church of Jesus Christ in the present age. They know that our children are the church's present moment—and that through the gift of this moment we may reach out to touch the next . . . and then the next.

The good news is that children enter our world with the same innocence and beauty and energy for life as they have in every other time. The good news is that we need them as much as they need us. The good news is that as we offer them a boost—just as we were once offered one for our climb—we participate in what is eternal. The good news is that there never has been and never will be anything greater than the unconditional love of God that embraces us all.

Scriptural Index